EFFECTIVE COMMUNICATION SKILLS

PSYCHOLOGY GUIDE TO IMPROVE CONVERSATIONS IN MARRIAGE, IN RELATIONSHIPS, IN BUSINESS MEETINGS AND IN PUBLIC SPEAKING. NON-VIOLENT COMMUNICATION SKILLS TRAINING

ANGELINA ZORK

Table of Contents

The trademarks that are used are without any consent, and the publication of the trademark is without permission or backing by the trademark owner. All trademarks and brands within this book are for clarifying purposes only and are owned by the owners themselves, not affiliated with this document.

The failure of a relationship is almost always a failure of communication.

(Zygmunt Bauman)

Introduction

Throughout your life, you are communicating with yourself, with others, or with the entire world. We use all that we have, be it through speech, writing, body language, and so on, to repeatedly flesh out mutually understandable meanings of what we think, how we feel, and what we perceive.

There are times when you can communicate clearly, whether through kind words, a sad frown, or a genuine laugh. There are also times when you unintentionally send out the wrong message when you mean something else, such as by responding with "I'm okay, "even though you feel completely uncomfortable. It is during these moments when you truly learn the importance of being able to communicate effectively.

The Context of Communication

"Communication" is the behavior that involves conveying intended messages from one communicator to another by employing mutually accepted and understood signs and symbols.

It has been observed that most–if not all– living beings communicate, but what makes human communication so distinct is its encompassing use of abstract language. This is what makes humans so complex because, through the millennia, we have been able to develop a wide variety of complex systems of communication to express our emotions, experiences, ideas, and perceptions.

Many scholars agree that three general human attributes have enabled us to develop sophisticated communication strategies. These are the Physical Attribute, the Cognitive Attribute, and the Social Base.

To understand the Physical Attribute, notice how you can easily manipulate your facial muscles to convey meaning, especially your mouth. Aside from that, your vocal apparatus (vocal cords, larynx, hypo larynx, tongue, teeth, and so on) enables you to produce a wide range of sounds. On top of that, you can create an almost boundless range of movements using different parts of your body to convey even more meanings. Without this attribute, our ability to communicate would be highly limited.

The Cognitive Attribute, however, is what truly separates human communication from other animals. Our cognitive abilities enable us to draw from experiences, essential thoughts, and ideas and then communicate them back to ourselves and others.

The third attribute, the Social Base, plays a crucial role in developing the mutually understood and accepted signs and symbols we use to convey our intended meanings. Without these interactions, there would be no spoken and written words and no complex language. Besides, the word "Communication" came from the Latin communicate, which translates as "to share."

Now, let us look at how these attributes play a role in human communication evolution.

The Evolution of Human Communication

Have you ever wondered how humans were able to develop a complex communication system? The following is a quick overview to give you an idea of how it all came to be.

Millions of years ago, humans began communicating with each other through expressive sounds and body language by using their Physical Attributes. These may include the uttering of grunts, shouts, and other patterns, and gesturing using one's hands, eyes, arms, and so on.

Because of their ability to fixate their mind on certain concepts (using their Cognitive Attribute), they continue to communicate with each other. They can also communicate with themselves using the same signs and symbols they have associated with the concepts. Thus, it is evident that the Social Base attribute plays an integral role in communication.

One of the most essential communication roles was to give names to certain objects, animals, events, and other important factors that play a role in human survival and culture. Thus, words to convey the meaning of night, day, rabbit, snow, cave, food, and other objects were conceived.

Eventually, the primeval human's' specific sounds and gestures are collectively understood to convey particular meanings. The collection of signs and symbols continues to expand because everyone repeats the same utterances and gestures. Also, they would then pass this elaborate system down to their offspring. However, as the number of utterances and gestures continue to grow, the ancient man found it difficult to rely on such a single word to convey different meanings. For instance, it would be difficult to rely on the mere symbol or gesture of the word "night" when one wished to say to his companions that they "will not hunt at night." You could only imagine how difficult it would be to rely on isolated words and gestures to express yourself then. Due to this growing need, an ancient man began developing a language structure within their society.

The need to keep records of ideas, experiences, and symbols further led humans to develop written communication. This system began with pictures painted on cave walls as the ancient man drew symbols of anything that have been chosen to fixate on, such as animals they hunted, lands they visited, etc.

A combination of different pictures to convey increasingly complex meanings then led ancient humans to discover the art of picture writing. However, drawing a wide variety of pictures to represent a single story was not sustainable for some cultures; thus, pictographic writing was developed. This was what the ancient Egyptians used as their system of written communication.

Another form of written communication was also developed, and researchers call it ideographic writing. This makes conveying spoken word into a written form more effective because it enables drawing abstract nouns such as truth, wisdom, and justice into symbols. The ancient Chinese characters are a perfect example of this type of writing.

However, to use pictographic and ideographic writing, one must memorize a continuously increasing number of characters representing even more concepts and visual symbols. As the ancient humans continued to interact with each other and their surroundings, it would not have been long before they became too burdened by the vastness of pictographs and ideograms. A more concise writing system must be created. Thus, alphabetic writing was created.

Alphabetic writing makes universal literacy a possibility because it enables the person to learn a specific number of symbols representing distinctive sounds instead of concepts. Putting these symbols together would enable the communicator to express the spoken word these symbols represent in written form.

As you can see, we have come a long way to where we are now, as far as communication goes. Each year, new concepts are formed, thus leading to the need to create new words. We no longer need to create new symbols to represent these words because of our fixed alphabet system. We now share our collective uses of these millions of signs and symbols through books, videos, telecommunications, and other informational media.

The Process of Communication

Now that you know a bit about the evolution of language, you must be curious to know how communication works. Well, linguists and other communication scholars generally agree that this process generally involves seven fundamental steps:

The first step is to construct the meaning you intend to communicate. This refers to the concept on which you have chosen to fixate your mind. For example, you are waiting in line at a coffee shop and looking at the menu board. Your mind remembers the good feeling you get from drinking a dark mocha Frappuccino, so you develop the communicative intent to order it.

The second step is to compose the message. You use your language skills to put together different words that would convey the conventionally accepted meaning you intend to communicate.

This leads to the third step, which involves the encoding and decoding of the message. You use your language skills to develop the best sequence of signals to convey your intended meaning. For example, you would think it conventional to say, "I'd like a dark mocha Frappuccino," to order the drink you want.

The fourth step is to transmit your sequence of signals that convey your encoded message using a particular channel. Besides verbal communication, which involves the auditory and verbal channels, the other communication channels are visual, tactile, haptic, kinesics, olfactory, biochemical, and electromagnetic.

In the coffee shop example, the channel would definitely involve the verbal and auditory channels. The receiver of your message would be the cashier of the coffee shop. As soon as you approach the cashier, you would then utter the message you had composed in your mind: "I'd like a dark mocha Frappuccino."

The fifth step is receiving the sequence of signals. In other words, it is now the turn of the cashier (receiver), who would acknowledge the message you expressed.

The sixth step is to reconstruct the original message. The cashier would interpret your message based on several factors, including her own physical and cognitive attributes and her language system, as formed by her social base.

The seventh and final step involves interpreting and making sense of the reconstructed message. If you both share similar, if not the same, language system, then she is most likely able to understand that you intend to order the dark mocha Frappuccino. However, if you both do not share the same language system, then a communication barrier would become present.

For example, if the cashier speaks another language and does not understand English, it would only be natural for her not to understand what you mean. Then, to help interpret and make sense of what you said, she would probably ask you to repeat or speak in French so that she would understand.

If the barrier continues to persist despite all efforts to use the verbal and auditory channels of communication, other non-verbal forms may be used. You might resort to pointing at the picture of the dark mocha Frappuccino, for instance. However, to show that you are not distressed, you continue to smile in a friendly way. As such, you are now using non-verbal communication. Through both parties' persistence, the barrier may dissolve, and both would understand the intended message.

Naturally, the ability to break down the barrier is easier done in some situations than in others. To increase your adeptness in communicating your intended meaning, you must make it a point to understand the different communication skills.

Chapter 1: Types of Communication

Four fundamental categories detail the most common types of communication used.

Verbal Communication

This method relies on words to communicate something. This is the standard way of communicating. The majority of people use this type of communication on a day-to-day basis. However, sometimes we use it without fusing it with other types of communication. Tone, motions, and non-verbal communication are just a few things people use while passing information. Observations, feelings, and opinions can be best communicated through verbal means. A conversation via the phone, catching up with a friend, or displeasure conveyed are mainly done verbally. It is easier this way for most of us.

When we were still children, we grew and learned verbal communication by listening and imitating the sounds around us. In a short while, we could understand languages and prompted us to speak verbally while growing. Verbal communication is additionally isolated into four portions:

Intrapersonal Communication

Intrapersonal communication consists of private talks that we have with ourselves, and we, generally, keep this to ourselves. However, there is the possibility that we inadvertently communicate what we did not wish to due to our body language, facial expressions, or other nonverbal cues.

Relational Communication: This is a one-on-one conversation where two people have to be sharing or holding a conversation. Relational communication is mutually beneficial—both individuals are senders and receivers of information, and both can understand one another well.

Small-Group Communication

This type of communication takes place when more than two people are involved. The number of individuals will be just enough that effective communication can still occur. Question and answer sessions, work meetings, and psychoeducational groups are a perfect example of this kind of communication. Unfortunately, miscommunication can arise in small groups, especially if the topics at hand allow room for disagreement. For example, a question and answer session might become heated if someone answers a question so that half of the group understands and agrees, and half of the group does not understand or agree.

In a typical organization, communication happens in the following ways:

Chain Flow of Communication

This is when someone who holds a "higher-up" position at a company needs to communicate a message to subordinates but cannot do so directly. Instead, they communicate it to the position just beneath them, who then communicates that message to the position just beneath them, and so forth. The message eventually gets to the workers who need to hear it, but it is often received as skewed or inaccurate because it was passed on so often.

By now, you might be asking yourself if chain flow of communication is such an unreliable mode of communication, why do organizations continue to use it? Below are a few examples of when a superior might need to utilize chain flow of communication to send a message to subordinates:

- Giving observations and criticism on how work has been done.
- Issuing work guidelines, corporate policies, and so forth.
- Giving a complete rundown to the workers on what is required of them to hit ion to targets.
- Communicating the organization's strategic vision or mission statement to every worker.

- Brochures, e-mails, and so on are examples of the written chain flow of communication. For effective and error-free communication, the superiors should:
- Indicate the main objective as clearly as possible.
- Guarantee a precise message, explicit and unambiguous.

Upward Flow of Communication

This is the kind of communication that is designed for a particular goal in an organization. Its objective is to inform the progress of the firm. The lower offices use this kind of communication to address issues and ideas to the offices above them.

Subordinates also use this method to inform the bosses on how well they understood instructions from them and seek clarification on issues that are not clear to them.

This type of communication process is designed to ensure the company is successful and creates faithful and committed employees, as workers need to have a voice within their employment place. The bosses are made aware of their feelings towards their directives, work, and the whole company.

Reports about the organization's position and reports on studies conducted in the company drafted by the employees and other external professionals also help this type of communication be more effective.

Parallel Communication

This is the kind of communication that takes place at the same level within an organization. This could look like communication among coworkers, supervisors, or CEOs—each of these groups communicates with others of the same work or professional status. The benefits of this type of communication are:

- Efficiency.
- Encourages positive challenges within the company.
- Gives real-time social collaboration to the individuals.
- It helps handle issues when they arise.
- It assists in the sharing of information.
- It can be utilized for finding solutions after disagreements between offices and individuals.

Diagonal Communication

This is the kind of communication that takes place when executives and representatives meet up. It doesn't show up on a hierarchical outline. For instance, the organization's budget planning or a specific branch or office under the organization and auditing of the funds.

External Communication

Communication takes place between someone who works directly with a company and someone who is not associated with that company—for instance, suppliers, banks, credit facilities, and so forth. The objective could be either to plan how the two organizations could work together in the future or any work that will benefit both companies.

Open Communication

This kind of communication occurs when one person communicates messages to groups of people who attend to receive those messages. Political rallies and religious gatherings are perfect examples of this specific kind of communication. In this instance, information is transferred from one source to the voluntary receivers of the information.

Non-Verbal Communication

This is a communication type that does not rely on words or sounds. It is the opposite of verbal communication. This kind of communication uses gestures, body language, facial expressions, and any other communication that does not rely on verbally spoken words.

Non-verbal communication could be viewed as a supplementary form of communication when used in conjunction with verbal communication.

Visual Communication

This type of communication incorporates the use of pictures or videos to transmit information. To understand the message being sent, one has to see the visual guides that are being showcased. For example, photos, signs, images, print outs, and maps are a few of the mediums used in visual communication. Movies, plays, and video television programs are the best in communicating visually. Visual communication can as well include information exchange as content electronically through telephones and computers. An Emoji can also be classified as a type of visual communication.

When symbols are utilized, they assist the reader and clients in understanding their importance in communication. The best example of this type of communication is the Web, which has several characteristics: a mix of pictures, words in shadings, different fonts, and graphs. These visual highlights demand us to see the screen and process the information to understand the message.

Media communication is creating at a transient rate to guarantee lucidity and to take out any uncertainty.

Written Communication

This kind of communication contains noteworthiness that is useful in different communication platforms. This communication is key when planning and executing a business module, as it helps improve data storage. In any case, writing can be unique in both formal and informal styles. The best writing style is when every writing factor has been considered before starting, and all the correct wordings are put to use. Another positive aspect to consider is that writing is more dependable on getting your point across. The message doesn't have an opportunity to change. The writer is forced to put together a complete thought before attempting to communicate.

It has the following advantages:

Written communication helps put down to paper the standards, principles, and rules that an organization uses in its operations.

It is a perpetual method for data sharing and comes in handy where records and documentation are needed.

It sets down the exact job descriptions where references could be made, unlike verbal communication, where one could easily forget and not have a point of reference.

Written communication is precise and to the point.

Well written communications can uplift the company's standards as compared to other organizations.

It gives readily available records for reference.

Written communication has some downfalls, as well, that include:

Written communication is costly as it entails too much paperwork and money to send the documents to the desired goals.

Replies and feedback from written communications are not instant as compared to other forms of communications.

Composed communication is tedious, and reactions not prompt. Writing and sending require more than just time but also money.

Effective written communications call for more knowledge and fluency in the language and understanding, as poorly written communications are prone to misinterpretation.

A lot of administrative work and message weight is included.

Composed or written communication is the type where words and sentences are used together to enable information to be passed on. Journals, diaries, phone text messages, organizational reports, magazines, and newspaper articles are some examples. In contrast to other communication types, composed messages can be corrected by the sender right before they are sent to the recipient making this an important factor in communicating both in official and casual circumstances. This type of communication outweighs other types, such as visual communication, especially when using electronic mediums; for instance, PCs, telephones, and other visual mediums such as televisions.

Chapter 2: Conversation through the Phone

One of the essential characteristics of achievement in business is the ability to converse by phone. Answering the handset is not a complex duty; however, using it in a business and specialized way is not easy.

Conversing with a client on the phone might often be a tricky mission. Without seeing a person's face, the messages might become mixed-up and meanings misread.

Disclose Your Identity

When people make calls, they should first introduce themselves. Start by revealing your name and talking with a fine tone. However, make sure to uphold your pitch level. People might not see the person with whom they are conversing. The caller should not use many passionate words at the beginning. So, it will facilitate to boost impressions regarding the caller and bring satisfaction for both parties.

Clarity

The caller must avoid speaking too quickly and mumbling. The receiver might not be conversant with the language used by the caller. As a consequence, it will assist the caller in putting across the message to the receiver correctly. Additionally, it will assist in reassuring the receiver.

Choosing Words

It is not correct to use the teenage language with the boss or grandfather. The caller should know the individual with who they are speaking. At times the caller might not know the person with who they are talking with. However, in the first phase of the call, the caller introduces themselves by revealing their names and title. Consequently, the caller should use their universal knowledge and apply appropriate language practices when conversing with other people over the telephone.

Listen Keenly

The receiver should listen appropriately and enthusiastically before answering the caller. Or else they might not answer correctly and get their message accurately. Additionally, when the receiver is listening to the caller over the telephone, they should not disrupt them. Generally, interrupting while somebody is speaking is considered an offensive practice.

Excellent and Expressive Language

People make calls to somebody to express their messages and get a response. As a result, individuals have to apply fine and explanatory language to make suitable discussion. Also, the language must be evocative and correctly flowing. Since language and tone is the only medium that people may utilize over the phone, it is appropriate to use excellent and descriptive language with meaningful information throughout the conversation.

Carry a Pen and a Paper

It is constantly best to utilize a pen and paper before and during a call. While making a call, both the caller and the receiver may have to note down something. It might be a phone contact or home address. The person making the call might have to waste their time and funds to buy a paper and a pen while calling, and it is not an excellent practice.

Utilize Speakerphone When Needed

It is easier for the caller because they might use their hands to multitask. On the other hand, it is like trying to listen to one voice through a hooted crowd of taxis for the receiver.

Use of Text Message to Communicate

Using phone messages to organize where an individual meets somebody is a common use of text messaging by many people. However, organizing a physical meeting with somebody is not carried out as regularly as calling. On the contrary, only a few people who send texts organize a meeting once a day.

Receiving and sending messages has one specific advantage as compared to voice calls. With the appropriate handset settings put in place, text messages may convey information silently between the sender and the receiver. The majority of people say they take advantage of generating and sending messages to the desired people noiselessly. On the other hand, very few people who send text say they do this daily.

As compared to voice calls, a moderately smaller number of people receive and send text messages for job purposes on their telephone. On the contrary, the majority of people rarely sent a work-related message. It implies that many work-related communications are channeled through voice calls.

Texting is less likely to be embraced for long conversations regarding individual matters than voice calls. On the other hand, text message users make distance calls to talk about a specific essential issue. On the contrary, a few people use messages for distance communication.

Not astonishingly, people who send and receive huge numbers of messages daily are likely to text regularly for all-purpose. This is as compared to the person who sends and receives fewer texts. In a comparable vein, people who make and receive high numbers of calls on their phones daily are expected to send and receive messages for several purposes.

For most categories of businesses, the phone plays a key part in daily operations. It is due to business persons needing them to contact dealers, business acquaintances, and clients. Phones are helpful because they enable communication with clients by permitting them to transact business-related activities at any time of the day. As vital as the telephone is, businesses must distinguish the difference between excellent and terrible phone etiquette. They must understand that how they call customers and business friends on the phone shall positively or negatively depict them. In the hands of a poorly trained worker, administrator, or company owner, phone communication might have a tremendously negative consequence on the business.

Receiving business calls at work comprises a different approach to a usual, non-business call. When clients call the company, they expect complete concentration. As a result, they do not desire to be kept waiting and need timely answers.

When a call is picked well, and clients are happy with the service, they will do business again. For a company, the phone is frequently the initial and only point of getting in touch with some clients. It might primarily make or break a company affiliation. That is why a lot of organizations employ specialized answering services nowadays.

Because opening impressions are permanent, and frequently such impressions are contacted on the phone, the client will judge the business by how the discussion went with the spokesperson. If the receiver can impress callers, then the company will have permitted clients to shop around. This implies that the company has given new customers a basis and an assurance to do business.

When a company spokesperson is prepared before taking a client's calls, it indicates a company's willingness to do business with the caller. On the other hand, keeping the clients waiting and speaking offensively might critically damage the company's status.

Phone etiquette is important in competitive business because if the company does not do it right, the client might choose from another alternative. Phone etiquette is an essential part of client service. Frequently, customers call for return business since they are familiar with how the company functions. If the receiver is not polite, timely, and well-informed, the company does not give the customer any reason to return.

Many people worldwide appreciate that their phones make them feel satisfied and help them get in touch with friends and relatives. On the contrary, many phone users express annoyance with their handset for the disturbance it generates.

Disadvantages of Using Phones at Work

Many upcoming companies have a vested curiosity in watching calls made during job hours. It might help decrease personal calls and offer information to coach workers on communicating with customers and business associates more efficiently. Creating a call-monitoring structure on a conventional land-line system is relatively easy.

However, it is not characteristically possible for small businesses to install such expensive equipment. The major shortcoming of phone communication is that it disrupts the workflow both in individual calls and job-related calls. It increases the view that the employees are constantly prone to accept calls at the expense of committing to work.

As every employee may agree, one of the difficulties of telephone calls of any sort is that they disturb whatever an individual is doing. Adding up cell phones to work adds one more disturbance. A worker who has to stop job tasks to respond to phones might suffer from reduced productivity during the day. It might cause the worker to ignore deadlines or put in additional hours to finish projects on time.

Employees who take job-related calls outside regular job hours, whether on a company-provided handset or an individual cell phone, might feel a disparity between their work and individual lives. That is one of the disadvantages of cell phone communication. It might be tricky for workers to enjoy time away from work when their duties fall over into family, communal, and break time. It might increase worker stress, reducing the capability of workers to manage job tasks successfully.

Chapter 3: Conversation to Non-Native People in Different Cultures

What Culture Has

Cultures are not just many. They are also diverse. A person in their daily life comes across many instances in which he invokes his sense of judgment by minding and balancing between factors; social, economic, environmental, etc. Working styles vary from place to place. Age, nationality, gender, race, ethnicity, and even sexual orientation can be considered a culture, but they will vary according to the prevailing circumstances.

People do not set out to create cultures. Cultures are a natural derivative of social interactions. That is, cultures are created through communication. Traditional literature is passed on to generations through communication. The characteristics of culture include roles, rules, laws, customs, and rituals. These aspects become imparted in how people communicate hence shaping their communication practice. And the resultant communication practice is perpetuated culturally.

Communication and culture do not only go hand in hand, but they are also interdependent. We start picking up our cultures at just around the same time we start learning to communicate. Also, when people from different cultures begin to communicate, they bring along their prior interaction behaviors. But as they get along, they begin to form their custom culture to identify and co-exist among themselves. That is why, for instance, company cultures differ, and relationships are unique.

Culture may be defined primarily as the set of uniquely shared values by a group of people. These values are absorbed subconsciously than they are imparted consciously. Once they begin developing in a person, they recognize what is normal and right versus what is strange or wrong. This resultantly influences how one thinks, acts, and keenly to be noted, the criteria by which they judge others.

We notably mention here that while people may be identified and described by their cultures, it is unjustifiable to define and judge them exclusively on that ground. Family upbringing, individual experiences, aspirations, education, and information can influence people's outlook and consideration of people and situations. At the core of the diversity that cultures present is the very natural desire to associate and cooperate with others and leave a positive mark.

Culture Considerations and Communication

High-Context versus Low-Context

Cultures can be considered to be high-context or low-context. High-context cultures encode and cast their communications into the context, while low-context extracts their communications from the context. High-context messages are more implied or indirect, while low-context messages are more express or direct.

In many corporate seminars today, the medium of communication is usually influenced by these contexts. It is not the degree of industrialization but the contexts that determine how people effectively communicate. This requires the speakers to be aware of the audience and try to communicate as much as possible appropriately.

In high-context cultures, personal bonds and agreements, though informal, are considered more binding than formal contracts. They operate on trust. Any meeting's intention is not necessarily for corporate reasons but personal bonding for a lasting connection and mutual interaction. Conversely, low-context communications prefer legal documentation in meticulous wording for any contracts or agreement to be considered valid. It does not matter the face behind a deal, as long as it is efficacious.

High-context communications leave more unspecified messages. The listener has to draw understanding from the context. The context includes cues and in-between-line hints. They generally find it disrespectful and disturbing to use certain words or associate with certain values and avoid exclusive communication words. The low-context cultures code their messages in an explicit and specific manner.

High-context cultures leave the meanings of their messages in what is not said. The listener needs to interpret body language, silences, pauses, relationships, and empathy, etc. For instance, when one wants something from you, you need to go your way to evaluate the details and provide for them even when not expressly mentioned. You do that because you mind your relationship with them and watch out for their welfare and success. The low-context messages are accurate and precise with detail, including timelines. It is about what is required, not about what one means to the other.

Time is Sequential or Synchronic

Cultures that consider time sequentially see it as a linear commodity to be spent, saved, or wasted. The past does not matter any longer as it is gone. The present must be optimally utilized to make the most out of it. Time saved is time created. Time wasted is irrecoverable, and a loss is incurred. The synchronic types consider time as always available and seize every moment to capture the full experience; however, much it takes.

The sequential types give exclusive attention to one thing at every moment until it is completed and then progress to the next. Focus for concentration, optimize for efficiency, and produce with promptness because that is how tasks will be completed faster and the next ones

40

initiated upon in their time. Time is money — the synchronic type work to have everything at the same time. To them, the past, the present, and the future are interdependent. So, if you plan anything, it must be the long term, not the short term.

You take the phone call while serving the client right before you and, at the same time, admiring the child playing with the toys in the waiting area. That is being synchronic. Perceived in this manner, it can be quite troubling how, for instance, they turn up for meetings. The sequential type considers lateness as a result of one who plans poorly and is disrespectful. The synchronic type finds the concept of timeliness as being childish impatience.

The sequential thoughts know that you can use personal effort today to influence the future. But since many dynamics affect the distant future, you take particular interest in the next quarter's results. If you feel results are at par with your expectations for the period, you are way on. The same principle works in relationships. Their existence depends on what you have done in someone's favor lately. The synchronic types consider the past to be the context to understand the present and prepare for the future. Relationships are the most important and durable thing, and the bonds established run back and forth in time. It is preferred to favor friends and relatives in dealings of business.

The Affective Versus the Neutral

The effects are the kind of personalities that readily show their emotions. If it does not add up, it is condemned, and the feeling of it must come out in a pronounced manner possible. If something is good and exciting, the affective will smile broadly and compliment using the best terms. The affective will grimace, smile, laugh or shout, cry, and

41

walk out, which offers them a solution. The neutral opt for the neutral approach to matters. It is not that the neutral does not feel, but they strive to keep their emotions controlled and subdued throughout their dealings.

The neutral is mindful of how much emotional display they make. They do not find it adequate to get excited or underwhelmed unduly. They focus on the task at hand and try to avoid personal distractions midway. The effective, on the other hand, prefer expressing their feelings openly. They get personal so fast and stop to engage rationally on the issue at hand. While the neutrals can get empathetic when their counterpart is upset, the affectionate once agitated care less. They relieve their emotions and leave you to soothe yourself.

The neutral believe every idea can work. It only needs to be so tested and, if approved, adopted for full implementation. The affectionate are opposites in this regard. They want facts and numbers at hand to decide on whether an idea can work or not. They try not to get involved deeper than they think they should. They draw boundary lines and go only that far.

However, you classify your culture, you will find that the differences are not necessarily just that, but a second thought will reveal how they are consistent. For instance, the fact that the synchronic strives to live and experience the moments to the fullest does not mean that they are not mindful of the future. At the same time, the sequential do not disregard the past. They learn from past mistakes and draw facts from past observations, for instance.

Generally speaking, no one lives exclusively by a certain culture's rules and totally disregards the others'. Is it possible the neutrals lose their patience after some time waiting? How about the affectionate sometimes managing their emotions in certain moments? The high-context cultures seem to share properties with the synchronic and neutral cultures and are more common among eastern continents. The low-context, sequential, and affective, common in the western world, seem to supplement each other significantly. This understanding of the macro-level dynamics can first inform how you respond to people at the first meeting and subsequently.

Cultures as Communication Barriers

Cultures shape mindsets, languages, signs, and symbols. The criteria for rating people and their values vary between cultures. Hence what one finds important might not mean much to someone else from a different culture. Different cultures with different languages encode and decode their messages differently and hence, may obstruct communication. Within the same languages, words may have different meanings depending on contexts, leading to misunderstandings. Also, signs and symbols, including body language and gestures, can differ and have varied meanings across cultures.

Stereotyping can be a major negative consequence of cultural differences. When preconceptions about people guide your interactions with them, then you are bound to provoke negative feelings that bar communication. When not well controlled by members, behaviors, beliefs, and religions can cause misconceptions by sending wrong messages. When one is unsure how to behave in a

43

stranger's presence from a different culture, they may become highly anxious. This anxiety might prevent them from initiating or responding to a conversation when prompted.

Cross-Cultural Communication

It refers to how people from different cultures communicate. It helps try to exchange and mediate between cultural differences through language, gestures, and body language. Try to listen more, or get an interpreter where possible so that you hear the exact real meaning of what is said other than the words in their plain meaning. Consider learning the elementary grammar of foreign languages and gestures of the cultures you interact mostly with.

Also, learn to become cognizant of your perception towards other people and make every effort to avoid prejudices and to stereotype. Accept differences and be open to learning from others. You cannot know everything. However, you communicate with people of other cultures, seek feedback, and open up to communication channels. Take charge of your emotions. Do not get in the habit of surprising others for not being considerate with your expressions of feelings.

When responding to people from a different culture, do so to provide the right response rather than the right message. Part of understanding their culture should be to consider how they take turns during a conversation. There surely cannot be one best suiting approach to communication between people. The success of it can only perhaps be in understanding and respecting the differences. It boosts creativity, teaches new perspectives, introduces new ideas, and contributes to world unity.

Chapter 4: The Magic of Communication in Marriage

It is quite unfortunate that the importance of communication is often not taken seriously in marriage. This is mainly because so many couples think daily banter or lack thereof does not affect them every day.

However, you must understand that communication is the engine that fuels all other parts of a marriage. If you love your spouse and fail to show them through words and actions, then the truth is that you are not doing right by them. If you genuinely love and trust them, then let them know how you feel about them. Communicating openly and with honesty ensures that your marriage stands a chance of flourishing and staying healthy. Communication must begin right from the time you are courting to marriage and into marriage.

When you and your husband or wife make effective communication the cornerstone of your marriage, you will enjoy a loving marriage. The only shortcoming is that there are people who are just not good at it. Having love, honesty, and trust is good, but they are not meaningful by themselves. It is by expressing these traits that yield a marriage that will become the envy of many.

The magic lies in showing love, acting honestly, and showcasing trust. Communicating how much your husband or wife means to you moves your marriage from good to high! The point is, expressing yourself goes beyond words alone.

Some of the benefits associated with effective communication in marriage include;

Minimizing confusion

Did you know that when you have been married to someone for 50+ years, you still cannot predict what is going through their mind? One of the biggest mistakes that couples make today is assuming that their spouse "knows." The problem with this kind of assumption is that your spouse may be thinking the complete opposite.

According to Eboni Baugh and Deborah Humphreys (Extension specialists at the University of Florida), it is critical that you clearly state your thoughts with utmost honesty to minimize confusion. Additionally, when saying your thoughts, do it positively as much as you can.

When you minimize confusion, what you are doing is increasing the commitment in your relationship. This commitment is what is directly related to satisfaction in marriage.

It maintains marriages through assurances

Satisfaction in relationships is directly correlated to the assurance that you give your partner. Marianne Dainton, a communications researcher, explains that assurance in marriage is what reaffirms you're the romantic desires of your partner. You can achieve this by choosing to use kind words and acts of love.

Other researchers report that couples who often engage in assurances often enjoy more significant commitment in their marriage, impacting their marital satisfaction positively.

Enhances marital satisfaction

When you are satisfied in marriage, you will live a healthier life, increasing your lifespan significantly.

However, if you are in a marriage characterized by poor communications, you will likely be caught up in a vicious cycle of poor, unhealthy conversations that contribute to dissatisfaction. When this cycle of poor communication is not corrected early enough, it has a likelihood of degrading your relationship.

Keeps a couple closer than they think

How do you know your spouse for who they are? Is there a way to know? You need to bear in mind that no one has a premonition or the power to read other mothers' minds. When we share our life's stories and experiences, we are certainly going to involve ourselves with others.

The same thing applies to marriage. Marriage is not just about physical contact; it is also about having an emotional connection with another.

When you share a little experience from your life with someone, however small it may be, this form of openness will surely draw you nearer to one another. It is what makes you both feel like one.

The only way you will know what is going through your spouse's mind and heart is by asking them. This is one of the best ways to resolve any issues that arise quickly and effectively.

Assumptions and misunderstandings are likely not to creep in

One of the things that we have mentioned earlier is that of making assumptions. But the most critical question is, how does communication in marriage ensure that assumptions and misunderstanding do not creep in?

We have to note that it is natural for one's mind to wander off and have the worst thoughts possible when they feel that their spouse does not share some specific information.

Think about a situation where you and your significant other speak to each other without any inhibitions. Will there be any form of negativity? Certainly not! The main reason is that you are ensuring that you close the door for assumptions. This way, you eliminate negativity from your life.

Once you know what you both like and dislike, beliefs, desires, opinions, and wants in life, you both will likely decide to see your marriage through to success. But the question is, "what do you think is holding you back?" Well, when you open your heart to someone else, this is indeed a blessing. The main reason is that you know that someone in this life knows and appreciates you for who you truly are.

Therefore, ensure that you are not keeping verbal gaps between the two of you to avoid the occurrence of disappointments and feelings of insecurities.

Communication reduces the occurrence of infidelity

Now, let's take a look at communication from a different angle. Ask yourself what communicating with others lead to. When did your spouse fail to share things with you that can be interpreted as not sharing their life with you, right?

It is important to note that when you keep things from your spouse, or even avoid a major conversation/argument and desire to be left alone, play a central role in breaking the bond you share. In other words, when you do this, you are pushing your spouse away.

In as much as this may not be the same case for all couples, lacking an emotional connection with your spouse may arouse the desire to make a connection with someone else. Trust me, you may not want to go down this path, but when your heart is not fulfilled with all of its needs and desires, it will strive to bring itself that satisfaction it wants.

Good communication demonstrates respect for your spouse through honesty

Have you ever found yourself in a situation where you do not wish to talk to your spouse, or your spouse does not want to talk to you and hence end the conversation right there and then?

Well, the truth is that this may work for you at least once or twice. However, over time, you may need to add in a few lies just so that you can get out of the situation. Note that, at this point, it is no longer avoidance; it is now backed up with a pack of lies!

The most important thing you need to note is that there is no need to introduce false information when there is nothing to hide from your significant other. This does because it destroys the chances of having a beautiful life you have always wanted with your spouse.

At first, it may start as an innocent thing to keep stuff from your spouse. However, with time, this kind of behavior highlights your lack of respect for them. It is high time that you become honest with them. At least that is what you owe them. They need to know what is going on in your life, mind, and heart so that you can both handle the situation and get ahead with life.

That said, you have to bear in mind that communication in marriage or any other relationship for that matter is a two-way street without any red lights. When you communicate with your spouse, it is much more than just sharing what you both have in mind. You cannot drop your frustrations, anger, and news at your spouse and then walk away like nothing just happened.

Understand that communicating simply means that you have to be present for each other. You have to be there when your spouse needs you to comfort them both physically and emotionally. Get over the belief that you just say what you feel and walk out of the room as a couple.

Opening yourself to your spouse means that you welcome the possibility of receiving information from them as well. In life, whether marriage or elsewhere, we all desire to be needed and wanted by someone. When you are there for each other in marriage, you will face problems and issues together. Nothing will be tough for you. There will be no argument big enough to threaten to break your relationship.

Indeed, communication is a process, but the most important thing is to learn that process so that it can bring you and your spouse closer. When you both learn how to communicate with each other, you develop a unique language. This is not to say that the process of learning effective communication is easy!

Trust me. It is hardly a natural skill. According to research, the quality and quantity of communication play a key role in bringing couples closer and improving marriages. Therefore, it is your responsibility as a couple to conduct experiments with various communication approaches and ensure that you make the process both fun and productive.

Importance of counseling before marriage

Suppose you are not yet married and are reading this book, bravo! This is a great step when preparing to get married. You have to understand that marriage is an exciting engagement that is often followed by a range of plans and activities for the wedding.

At this point, much of the details of your communication may take a focus on the wedding. If you are not careful, the wedding may take the place of even much more important discussions about your future as a married couple. When you seek marriage counseling ahead of your marriage, you are simply increasing your chances of enjoying a satisfying union together. Yes, you may have fallen in love with each other, but you have to understand that a happily ever after takes lots of effort and preparation!

Marriage triangle

Three major factors constitute a marriage triangle. These factors include; couple traits, individual traits, and context of the relationship.

Based on a study conducted by Jeffrey H. Larsen on marriage preparation, such individual traits as self-esteem, beliefs, and interpersonal skills affect how one approached marriage. Understand that expectations are not everything! However, they affect everything.

One thing that you need to bear in mind is that marriage counseling brings into focus expectations. It is about bringing them to the table for discussions to ensure that problems are kept at bay.

Some of the couple's traits that play an important role in marriage include their goals, values, communication, and conflict resolution skills. With the help of a marriage counselor, a couple can build on their strength and develop various ways of overcoming their weaknesses. Realize that your contexts and your relationship constitute some of the baggage you bring with you from your past. One of the best ways to deal with these issues is to have an objective third party before crossing the threshold.

Chapter 5: Communicate with Children. Social Anxiety in Children

How We Can Help Them

Children experience anxiety differently than adults. Adults at least have a simple understanding that their bodies are experiencing something; children aren't as fortunate. They are still learning their bodies and all the different feelings that come with it. We need to notice the changes in them so that we can help them work through it. Changes that children go through, like changes in routine, can enhance their anxiety. Finding ways to help them through it is important to learn self-regulation at a young age.

- Startle easily
- Clinginess
- Crying uncontrollably
- Tantrums
- Poor sleep
- Headaches
- Stomach aches

These are common symptoms of anxiety in children. Not all anxiety is bad, but it is important to be able to identify it in children. Chances are your child isn't just throwing a tantrum because they don't want to be dropped off at daycare. It could be signaling to you that they are going through anxiety about the situation. Here are the common types of anxiety seen in children:

Separation anxiety

Separation anxiety is something that a child can go through when they fear being away from their parents. They have an uncontrollable fear that something may happen while they are away from this parent, so they do not want to leave their side. This can hinder them from experiencing social milestones like sleepovers, camps, or playdates.

Social anxiety

Much like adults, children can feel the effects of social anxiety. They may fear going to new places or being around many people because they fear being judged or humiliated.

Specific phobias

These are things that specifically cause anxiety in a child. Things like insects, weather phenomena, and the dark are examples of specific things that can cause a child immense fear and anxiety.

Even though normal anxiety levels are okay in a child, talk to their pediatrician if you notice that their anxiety symptoms seem to be limiting their activities. Extreme levels of anxiety can delay or derail a child's development. There are a lot of therapies that can help a child who is experiencing anxiety. Cognitive-behavioral therapy is popular among children because it allows them to participate in their child's therapy. Mindfulness approaches have also been helpful with children, and there are medications available to help with the anxiety. Your pediatrician will figure out the best defense line for your child if you suspect they suffer from anxiety.

How Parents Can Help Their Children Manage Anxiety

As a parent, you are an advocate for your child. You want to help your child in any way you possibly can, and there is nothing wrong with that. You can take steps to help your child understand their anxiety and ways to help them learn to manage. This is a better approach if you prefer not to seek a medicinal route, and these things will probably be covered by a pediatrician as well.

Personalize and externalize

Have your child name their anxiety. Let them draw pictures to represent this anxiety. This can help your child learn to face it without being scared of it. It can also help them express to you when this "monster" comes around.

Preview potential situations

Try to introduce your child to new places and people ahead of time if possible, which will reduce the anxiety they may have when entering the situation for the first time.

Show confidence

Children can easily read your emotions. Try to pay attention to your own emotions to not become agitated by your anxiety if it were to arise. Talking to them about your anxiety may help them understand their own,

Narrate the world

Children's brains are sponges. They are learning about their surroundings all the time. If they believe that someplace is not safe, more than likely, they are going to associate anxiety and fear with that place from now on.

Allow distress

Avoiding situations that trigger anxiety in a child only causes anxiety to pop up somewhere else. You have to allow your child to feel the distress and help them work through it using coping mechanisms so that it isn't as hard for the next time.

Practice exposure

Gradual exposure to an anxiety trigger in a child can help them come to terms with the fact that they can survive anxiety. In some instances, it can even show a child that they can overcome their fears in situations.

Anxiety in Teenagers

Your teenager is a mysterious being living in your house. Hormones have been a little crazy for years now, and sometimes they want to talk to you, and sometimes they don't. Simply put, it is hard to read the teenage mind and know what is going on in it. They are beginning to date, and they are working hard in school, playing sports, or even holding down a job. All of these things are raining down on your teenager, but they aren't comfortable enough to share things with you, and even though you want to help them, it may make you uncomfortable, so you just leave it alone.

Look for emotional changes.

Some teenagers may feel excessive worrying while others may exhibit other symptoms like feeling "keyed up," feeling on edge, extremely irritable, difficulty concentrating, restlessness, or unexplained outbursts. They may not have control over some of these issues, so it is important to keep an open communication line if you start to notice these changes in your teenager.

Take note of social changes.

Anxiety can put a strain on the friendships of your teenager. Even if your teen was once a social butterfly, it is important to note that abrupt changes in their social interactions. If they start to avoid their usual friends, avoid extracurricular activities, isolate themselves, or spend more time alone, it might be time to talk to them and see if they are going through something. It could be a phase, but it could also be anxiety.

Physical changes

Often, when there are changes in your teenager's physical symptoms, it could be nothing more than a cold, but it could also develop something more serious. If they are experiencing headaches that worsen in frequency, stomach problems, unexplained aches and pains, extreme tiredness, not feeling well without a medical cause, or changes in their eating habits, it may be a sign that they are suffering from physical changes brought on by intensifying anxiety problems. See a doctor if you feel like this is a possibility so that your teenager can get the proper nutrition help that they may need.

Changes in sleep patterns

It is recommended that teenagers should be getting between eight and ten hours of sleep a night. They should be shutting their screen time down thirty minutes before bedtime so that their minds can properly shut off. It is completely normal for homework, social engagements, and extracurricular activities to play a role in the sleep patterns of teenagers, but if you are noticing increasing issues with your teenager falling asleep, staying asleep, not feeling refreshed after the recommended eight to ten hours of sleep or increasingly vivid nightmares it is possible that their social status is not the reason for their sleep troubles. It is possible to try something like melatonin and create sleep rituals for them, but if it becomes too big of a problem, seek medical attention.

Performing poorly in school

Considering that anxiety can affect anything from sleep to diet, it is possible that with those contributing factors, your teenager could be performing poorly in school because of their anxiety. Often, anxiety causes kids to miss school because of their fear of being around people. Things to keep an eye on with your teenager is a significant jump in grades, frequently missing assignments, expressing that they feel overwhelmed by the workload, and procrastinating on projects and homework more than usual.

It is possible that your teenager has been experiencing anxiety for a while but has kept this from you. They may not know how to process the information themselves, or they are simply embarrassed by it. Make sure that you are keeping an open line of communication with your teenager. Sometimes it is hard to break the ice with them, but here are some tips on how you can accomplish this:

Empathize

Even though your teen wants to be independent, they also want to be validated and understood. When your teen brings on the line that something is ridiculous or illogical, this is when you can show them that you understand because you were once in their shoes. Try showing them that you know their feelings and that you are there to help them through what they are going through. It doesn't hurt for them to see you as cool in this, either.

Relate

Let your teenager know that they aren't alone in this. Let them know anything that you have or are going through that might be closely related to their situation. Sharing your struggles and insecurities with them might help them open up to you as well. Let them see you as someone who can understand them and rest their notion that adults could never know what they are going through.

Ask

If your teenager seems to be struggling, simply ask them about what they are going through. Let them know that no matter what the situation is, they can talk to you. Ensure that they know that they open up to you that you will keep your cool and not judge them no matter what. The idea of judgment for them is as bad as the anxiety itself. They need to know that they can turn to you when the situations they are going through are too much to handle.

The most important thing you can do for your teenager right now is to let them know that all of this is normal. Let them know that they are not "crazy" because right now, there is a chance that they feel like they might be. They do not understand completely what is going on with them, and they need some insight. Ensure that you are reminding them as much as you can that you are willing to openly talk about anything they may need to open up about and that there is no judgment involved. Stopping the anxiety cycle early can make for more natural adulthood for them.

Chapter 6: Conversation at Work

Let's start by observing that just as every individual, and every group conversational dynamic, is unique, every workplace is unique also. Maybe you work at a white-collar financial firm, or perhaps you work at a social service agency, or it could be your work in a fast-paced food service establishment. Each of these work environments will have their own set of established cultures, with their own set of expectations of how each worker should behave within that culture.

Your first task, especially if it's your first week on the job, is to figure out what that culture is. What's generally considered appropriate and what isn't. You do this by using your basic conversational skill of honesty, good listening, and positivity. What constitutes an inappropriate remark or question? To what degree do I feel free to share my personal life? What is strictly verboten? There are some simple rules; however, that applies to virtually all workplaces.

We'll first observe that the workplace is different. It's not your home, and it's certainly not that bar where you hang out with friends after work, though a few of those friends might very well be coworkers.

Yet, the majority of all your conversations in life will happen in the context of work. And, of course, how well you perform at work will determine in great measure your degree of success in life. We're not just alluding to possible financial rewards, though they're important, to be sure. If you're spending over half your time at work, as so many of us do, we have to factor in the quality of that time as the primary measure of success. Are you happy and content? Are you considered a valuable member of the enterprise? Do you go to work every day with a pleasant expectation? Or is it just drudgery you dread the moment you wake up until the moment the day is over?

The difference between these two possibilities is often the quality of the personal relationships you format your work. And that depends on a very high degree on your conversational skills. Workers like coworkers who make them feel good about themselves. Mastering the art of conversation will help get you there.

Workplace Basics

It's not surprising that people who are successful in their workplace are effective speakers. Let's start with three basic observations:

- The same principles apply in the workplace as they do in all conversations. Always be honest, listen carefully, and with a positive attitude.

- Speak clearly and always to the point. Use appropriate jargon as a shortcut when necessary, but always be clear who your listeners are. There will be people you'll deal with that don't have your specific expertise within most workplaces. Strive to use the language they will understand.

- Don't waste people's time! Don't turn a brief discussion into a twenty-minute monologue. Sure, you want people to like you. You'll get better results if your comments are polite but to the point. They want to look good at work too. You help them by being a professional.

This last point deserves a little more explanation. But this isn't the time. And now you're feeling a little resentful.

Don't be that person! This doesn't mean you should be Ms. Perfect and Ms. Above-It-All. In the workplace, there's a time and place for such chit-chat. It's called break time. The workplace is different, and sometimes you have to prioritize the professional obligation over the social obligation. You need to tell your friend, sorry, l have a deadline, but let's get together for lunch. I saw the show too.

What you just did was communicate. One of the most important things we do in any workday is keeping our coworkers informed. But it's a professional environment. You might let out when you sit down to get that report done that you've got a deadline by noon. That's not an invitation to ponder the nature of deadlines. It's a signal to your coworkers not to bother you unless necessary. Later, after you've handed in your report, it might be useful to thank those around you for giving you the space to get that work done. You've set a boundary, but you've done it in a useful and positive way.

The Big Job Interview

This is where the stakes are highest, and your new conversational skills will be most useful. The first and most important point is don't get stressed over what you don't control, namely whether you'll get the job or not. It's not your decision. What is within your control is how you'll conduct yourself. Your conversational skills will help you in your conduct.

- Be open and honest about yourself. Try to appear relaxed and comfortable.
- Explain what you can do for your prospective employers.
- Listen attentively and with curiosity.
- Be polite but don't be overly flattering.

People want to work with someone they feel comfortable with. If you appear at ease - not slunk down in a chair, of course – though alert and present, you're passing the very first test. Don't be stiff, but try to be tuned into the moment. When people recognize someone who's 'open,' they tend to feel relaxed. This is often the deciding factor when an employer has to decide between equally qualified applicants. They just liked you more.

Prepare in your mind ahead of time a few key points about how your background and personality will specifically apply to the position.

Don't be bashful, but don't be cocky. Just state the facts. Also, show that you've done some homework by being familiar with some key issues the organization faces. Explain how you can help them meet specific goals.

Be prepared to ask specific questions. This shows your seriousness. You've already given considerable thought to the position. And don't hesitate to ask questions, but make them thoughtful. Show your curiosity and open-mindedness in this manner.

Maybe flattery will work, though it probably won't, but you want to get the position on your own merits. Here you're using honesty. You're yourself. You don't want to take a position under false assumptions regarding who you are. It would be exhausting to go to work each day, trying to remember what they hired would do every little thing. Also, genuineness just shines through. Again, people like people who are comfortable with themselves.

Conversation with Subordinates

A general principle of good conversation applies here, perhaps even particularly so. Talk with those you've tasked with supervising strictly you'd want your boss to speak with you. Your subordinates are, in fact, a reflection of you. Your peers and supervisors will form opinions about you based upon their opinions of you. And there's no hiding ill-will. It always comes out one way or the other.

Be generous with your praise but don't avoid unpleasant conversations either. This starts with communication that is always open and honest. Clearly expressed expectations are the best thing you can give any employee. A sure way to win respect is always to give them a chance to express their own opinions and listen to them carefully and with an open mind.

And never speak ill of one employee to another. Not only does it undermine respect for you, but it also creates a long-lasting resentment that will cloud and complicate all your dealings with all your colleagues going forward.

Conversation in Meetings

Almost nothing will shape your coworkers' opinions of you more than how you handle yourself in meetings. This is where your conversational skills are put to the ultimate test and where they can prove most beneficial. Whether you're leading the meeting, a key participant, or sitting on the sidelines, there are a few basic guidelines to follow.

First and foremost, even if you're the lead, the meeting isn't about you. The meeting will have a clear purpose, and everything said, except for the most basic pleasantries, should be said towards the end of achieving that purpose. Here's where you can shine, and here's where less is often more. The well-chosen few words at the right time can often be the decisive factor in making the meeting a success rather than a failure.

Listen, listen, and listen. Even if you're the guy presenting, while you're presenting, be aware of the signals being given off. When you're done, be done. Don't be overly defensive but try to engage others and listen to them carefully, honestly. To do this requires patience, of course, but that's why they're paying you the big bucks—or paying you at all, perhaps.

If you're not the presenter, but a participant expected to chime in, then chime in briefly and to the point. Make sure your opinion is clear but not to the point of inflexibility. Meetings are all too often where office politics become open warfare. Try to avoid becoming anyone's enemy combatant. Remember, the meeting has a clear purpose, and it's usually not to make someone look bad. Try always to limit your comments to achieving that purpose. Strive to be the person people want at the meeting, the solution-giver, and not the problem-maker. This is usually achieved with fewer words said than more digressions gone into.

Workplace Conversational Don'ts

There's no reason to keep secret your religion. It's part of who you are, so it's perfectly okay to mention things you do to celebrate. But be aware that not everyone worships how you do. It's a good rule of thumb not to discuss your religious beliefs in detail. And never share negative opinions about others' beliefs. And don't ever, no matter what, proselytize at work.

Politics is undoubtedly a loaded topic these days. It seems to make people crazy and has even ended a few marriages. Given the amount of time you spend at work and the need to get along and work with your colleagues, going there just isn't worth it and will only cause hard feelings between you and them.

Sex. Not only might you get suspended and terminated on the spot, but it could also get you into long term legal trouble. The conversation about sex is the big no go zone. If someone feels intimidated or if you've created an offensive work environment, he or she can wreck your life. Save it for your friends well away from your workplace.

Discussing family problems is generally a bad idea for several reasons. First, you might cause others to wonder if they're distracting you from your job. Even if they're not, they might not know that. When managers reveal things about their problems, their subordinates might see this as a weak spot and try to exploit it. This can undermine your authority and maybe fire up the rumor mill and make you the object of gossip.

There nothing wrong with seeing your job as a stop on the way to better jobs. Please keep it to yourself, though. Talking about it will undermine your employee's respect for you and make your boss question your loyalty. Nothing good ever comes of it. If you want to advance, do a great job, be an asset, and be the person people enjoy working with. Your boss will see that your time and each day will be enjoyable and rewarding even if you don't move up.

Chapter 7: Bonding with Colleagues

Can you imagine what life in the workplace would be like if everybody were hostile to everybody else? Nothing would go on, right? Thus, colleagues need to form tight professional relationships. Once colleagues have a favorable attitude toward one another, it becomes far easier to reach milestones and accomplish company objectives. The following are some of the practices that strengthen the bond between colleagues:

Know your colleagues

It may sound obvious, but not many people follow observe the tip. It's common to find workers ignoring each other and burying themselves into their tasks, with a "Don't disturb" attitude written all over. But this is usually the first step toward establishing tight bonds. Workers ought to approach other workers and want to know about them. It is in no way a violation of their privacy but just an effort to get to know their coworkers. This problem appears to be common in this generation. When technology was at the infant stage, people of long ago didn't have gadgets to offer them an escape window from reality, and they had no choice but practiced their social skills. But in the current world, it is unsurprising to find a whole adult with zero communication and social skills. But back to the point, people ought to be active in knowing about their colleagues and creating close ties.

Do you share common interests?

When two people share a common interest, they are likely to become too fond of one another. It's a biological thing. We are wired to react positively toward the people that share our traits. Thus, if you want to capitalize on this factor, take the risk and go asking around what they like doing. Should you come upon someone that shares your interests, it means you have a bigger potential of establishing close ties with them. But be sure that you don't sound like a spy. It has to be subtle, and if they resist, then back off, only to ask some other day again. Some of the subtle ways to ask a colleague about their interests include: noticing their recent wardrobe addition, their recent shoes, smile, and energy levels.

Develop trust

Every rewarding relationship is founded on trust. A professional relationship ought not to be different. You should start by showing other people that you trust them. For instance, you can leave money and other possessions in an area that your colleagues can see. Do they tell you about it, or do they keep mum? This is a corrupt way of finding out who's to be trusted or not. But it is essential to have a close-knight group of colleagues where everyone feels equal. Relationships are work, and it takes many sacrifices to make an office group tight and dependable.

Be positive

When you are preparing your work relationships, you have to be a person that constantly spits out positivity. People need to have a positive mindset for a relationship to flourish. Being positive is simply focusing on the bright side of things. Positive people are aware that they hold power, and they don't indulge in self-inhibiting tendencies. But they act with confidence, as they go for their important life goals. Positivity is like a muscle. You have to replenish it on the regular lest you slip. Engage in activities that build your positive energy and make better utilization of your free time.

Support your colleagues

This is perhaps the greatest hurdle that colleagues have to face. It is relatively easy to have everyone's cooperation when doing something for the company. Still, when it comes to supporting an individual's personal goals, there's nearly no enthusiasm on the part of colleagues. Of course, it reflects poorly on workers. Workers should be their own biggest supporters! If one of you has a project, find a way of giving it a boost, and invest in your colleague's success story. Obviously, this is a tall order because most people are selfish and want to engage in things that directly benefit them.

Share

To strengthen your professional relationship with other colleagues, you must get into the habit of sharing. You have to share ideas, plans, and even stories. This habit promotes integration, and the more you spend time together, the tighter your relationship becomes. It would be best to focus on sharing positive things to draw inspiration from that and improve their lives. In this advanced technology age, you can share messages in various formats like videos and even put categories to these messages. Ensure that you label them for easy retrieval.

Work on your social skills

This is an area that people at the workplace need to really invest in. human beings are social animals. We tend to respect those who can fit in within our social structures. But then there's so much nervous energy floating around whenever people do a simple meet up. Does it mean that most of us lack social skills? Certainly! But the good thing is that social skills aren't inborn traits. Anyone can acquire these skills as long as they practice. The biggest way – and the most challenging nonetheless – of developing social skills is forcing yourself to attend more social functions and taking part.

Avoid cliques

Cliques are so high school. They should not be tolerated in the workplace. In the workplace, most people are presumably mature and maybe aren't desperate for validation. But when colleagues start breaking themselves off into cliques, it signifies a lack of team spirit. A truly united team wouldn't break off into cliques. All workers should be free to interact with whoever they want to. And being able to share with anyone in the group is one of the things that will strengthen the team spirit. Cliques also incite unnecessary competition and, in some instances, even conflict. You had better steer away from cliques.

Work on your mental health

Mental health stats are worrying. Up to 40% of Americans are battling some form of mental illness. And this doesn't even capture the real horror of it, considering that most Americans don't seek professional help for their mental health challenges. Being in any form of relationship with a mentally ill person can be a real challenge. Their struggles have caused them to have a skewed perception. Thus, expect constant fights with them, considering that their perception of reality will be flawed. But mental health troubles can be overcome. Once someone accepts that they need help, the next step is to get them qualified personnel to help them recover.

Stop whining

Whiners receive no love; colleagues hate them, and management has no time for them. Thus, you had better become good at handling your issues without involving the entire world. A whining person might have legitimate troubles, but their horrible attitude, coupled with impatience, makes it hard to help them. Ensure that you aren't whining to either colleagues or bosses. It discourages people from forming partnerships with you as they fear you will take off whining again. To stop whining, you must acknowledge that the world is a jungle and that the fun is overcoming our existential problems.

Practice honesty

If you want to cultivate strong ties with your colleagues, learn to be honest. For some crazy reason, we are so used to telling lies that we even tell needless lies. Telling lies is an indication of insecurities and low self-esteem. Understand that you are competing with yourself. It's a world of billions of people. And it doesn't matter what position you are in because someone else will always be in a better or worse situation. For honesty to become your second nature, you have to get rid of unrealistic expectations, for they are a burden, and start observing more. If you have a reputation as an honest person, then everyone will want to work with you.

Thank people

If someone lends you a helping hand, they'll be curious to see whether you are appreciative or entitled. An appreciative person takes the time to express their gratitude. But an entitled person cannot bring themselves to say "thank you" for, in their skewed mindset, they are royalty. So, the little favor someone did for them, oh, that was to be expected!

Chapter 8: Facing Problem with a Right Communication

In as much as it can be easy to get communication right, it is also equally easy to get things wrong. Sadly, the latter is more likely to happen in one's day-to-day.

The Barriers towards Effective Communication

Whether he is conscious of it or not, man has several barriers erected around him to prevent messages from being interpreted the way they should be.

By identifying what these barriers are, you are one step closer to improving your communication skills. After all, what is there left to do with a barrier that you identified than to, well, smash it?

Physical Barriers

This is the one easiest to spot because it depends on actual physical conditions in the environment. For instance, you are trying to talk to a person, but they are several meters away from you. Or what if you are trying to talk to somebody in a crowded, noisy room?

Even the layout of an office can serve as a barrier to effective communication. For example, cubicle walls can absorb a lot of noise, which prevents workers from talking to each other unless they stand up and talk with each other over the wall.

And, of course, faulty equipment is a physical barrier, especially in remote communication. A broken microphone or a sudden weakening of the Internet connection can cause distorted messages, preventing listeners from interpreting a message properly.

Fortunately, being easy to spot means that physical communication barriers are the easiest to solve. If one can't hear you because you're too far away, you get closer to the listener. If the walls in your office are preventing communications, you talk over them. And if your communication equipment is faulty, then you invest in newer and more reliable ones. And so on.

Language Barriers

You will also encounter a linguistic barrier often, but it is a bit trickier to deal with. The fact that each region of the world has their own preferred set of languages can be a barrier to effective communication because two people may not know how to talk to each other in one language that both know.

"But isn't English the universal language now?" you might ask. That is true. Ever since the world has become globalized, many countries have adopted English as the standard for international communications.

But here is the thing: English is not the same in one country over another. For instance, the kind of English used in America is completely different from the one used in Britain or Canada. The same goes for other continents that have their own colloquial terms used in conjunction with English words.

On a more local scale, the dialects change from one region to another or, more accurately, once every few thousand kilometers. Of course, some nationalities speak English with a rather thick accent.

Included here are the different linguistic styles. Some people speak in a simple and yet direct manner while others are very lengthy and use highfalutin words. Then, those professions encourage people to talk at an advanced English level like law, academics, and science.

As a result, in one modern neighborhood, you can find more than three dialects, accents, and linguistic levels used in daily communication.

Psychological Barriers

This is one of the more insidious barriers as you will not know that they exist until they manifest themselves. The most common psychological barrier is stage fright, where you experience massive nervousness before speaking in front of several people. If overwhelmed by their nerves, the person may even experience difficulty delivering a single sentence clearly.

But there are far more potent psychological barriers being erected around people out there. These include depression, speech disorders, phobias, and other deep psychological problems that limit one's ability to speak clearly.

In most cases, some psychological issues collaterally affect your speech only. This means that fixing them must be done not only to improve your communication skills but to improve your mental health as well.

Emotional Barriers

Although closely related to psychological barriers, emotional barriers have a shorter lifespan. In other words, they are barriers only because of your emotional state at that moment made them so.

A strong emotional quotient allows a person to communicate effectively and perceive how their speaker intends for them to be received. However, high emotional states can affect your way of receiving messages.

For example, anger and sadness can make a person interpret a message negatively. On the opposite side of the spectrum are happiness and contentment, making a person even more receptive to messages.

Cultural Barriers

A more recent barrier faced by people is the exposure to different cultures coming from different nations. It cannot be helped that one culture is different from yours, and such differences can be manifested by the way you communicate with them.

People coming from reserved, isolationist cultures tend to speak only when spoken to. Those coming from more open and highly social cultures tend to be easy conversationalists.

Other cultural factors consider a religious practice or lack of one, sexual identity, diet, preferred pets, and overall general behavior. And this might even surprise you, but cultural factors will also dictate the type of topics you can expect to talk about when it comes to certain cultures.

As such, it is a must to consider the differences in cultures when communicating with other people. You cannot assume that they will perceive things the same way you do due to these differences. This is the very essence of being culturally appropriate.

Attitude Barriers

The way that a person is predisposed towards interpersonal interactions will also determine how well they communicate with others. Introverts like to be left alone and thus shy away from most verbal communications and physical contact. However, they might excel in remote communications like online chatting.

And then there are those personality types that are social or clingy. Of course, personality types could be perceived as blunt and inconsiderate or egotistical and domineering. All of these could play into how you can communicate with people. Under the right conditions, they could even serve as an impediment to getting your message across properly.

Organizational Barriers

This barrier is commonly seen in places where there is an organizational structure. Here is a scenario: have you ever wanted to talk to a person but feel hesitant because they are one rank or several ranks higher than you in the company's organizational chart? That's an organizational barrier.

Or what if you wanted to tell a person something but can't because company protocol demands that you do not disclose sensitive information to people lower in the chart? That is an organizational barrier right there.

Admittedly, many companies are doing away with the organizational charts' rigidity and employ a more transparent line of communication between people regardless of their position. This means that how much the organization's structure can impede communications depends greatly on that group's culture.

One Important Reminder: Although these barriers are prevalent, it does not mean that you will have to face all seven of them even in your lifetime. If you are a person who has never traveled to another country, you may have never had a linguistic barrier problem. And if you know how to circumvent them, physical barriers might not even be a problem for you.

Also, the magnitude of the problems that one faces is different from another person. Your psychological barriers might be minor compared to another person, but you might have more problems dealing with organizational barriers than those around you.

The point is that knowing what barriers you have to face in your communication skills is the key to finding a way to discover a creative workaround for problems they might pose.

Busting Some Misconceptions

As with any other skill out there, it is easy to build your communication skills on the wrong foundations. Such foundations are based on some misconceptions regarding the art of conveying your thoughts and feelings to others. As such, we must correct such wrong information to proceed properly.

Myth 1: Listening Skills are not needed

This myth is based on the notion that communication is simply relaying your thoughts and ideas to another person and nothing else. As such, you only need to learn how to craft your message to be a good communicator.

But the truth is that it only makes you a good talker, not a communicator. Listening is an essential skill to learn, as it helps you form your words in response to how people are feeling or most likely will receive your message. In essence, good listening skills help you refine your message and make it resonate with whoever you are conversing with.

Myth 2: Sharing of Information is the same as Communicating

The truth is that communication is always a dialogue, not a monologue. This means that more than one person is involved, and a back and forth of responses are to be expected if an interaction is to be labeled as a conversation.

Communication focuses on the two sides between participants, which means that a considerable focus is placed on maintaining a healthy conversation with people. In other words, your ability to read non-verbal cues, process responses, and adjust your way of talking accordingly are crucial skills to become a better communicator.

Myth 3: You Must Only Share the Message in One Way for Optimum Effect

Here is the thing about humans: they won't get what you are trying to say at once. This is dependent on whatever barriers they have inadvertently erected for themselves that prevent such a message from being processed properly.

As such, you need to find ways to make your message reach out to many people. This can be done by finding the right platforms to air out your message and the type of form it will take. For instance, if you have a good speech, you can convert it into text form for easy reading or make it a supplement to a lecture.

It's up to you to find out how you can keep your message "evergreen" for as long as possible.

Myth 4: Constant Communication is Always Good

Sure, talking regularly is one way to improve your skills. After all, practice makes perfect.

However, as with all things, the best signifier that you have improved as a communicator is not quantity but quality. There are a lot of people out there that talk a lot without saying anything meaningful. And then some say important things but keep repeating them.

Frequency is also a matter that you need to figure out in delivering your message. Say it too many times, and it might become annoying; say it sparingly, and it won't have an impact. The right amount of repetition for your message, while also keeping its form diverse enough, should help make whatever you are trying to say last in the minds of listeners for as long as possible.

Chapter 9: Skill to Communicate One Emotion to Other and Oneself (Self-Awareness)

Communication proceeds with emotions. Whatever statements we make take a part of us or affect us in a way or the other. There are situations, however, in which emotions can get stronger and more pronounced. One has to use a more conscious effort to stay on the communication course without being distracted. Emotions, both positive and negative, can influence one's judgment.

While negative emotions make one utter negative statements without due realization, positive emotions can entice one to make commitments that they would rationally have avoided. Thus, one must be careful not to exhibit their full-scale weaknesses—the mind reasons by thoughts and the body by emotions. When the latter takes precedence, then a communication breakdown inevitably looms.

So how can you take charge of your communications in emotionally charged situations?

Emotional Intelligence

It is important at this stage to regard what emotional intelligence means in communications. Success in any technical, social, and business ventures is associated more with the person's emotional intelligence than mental intelligence. An expert who cannot handle their feelings will lack the virtue of sticking to something to the end. But a novice who shows willingness and commitment to the same activity will soon get it done exceptionally well.

Thus, it is not just what one knows about something, but more importantly, how they handle themselves at it. That gives meaning and value to the whole process and the result of it. The same is the case with communication. A manager who easily gets angry or frustrated working at something is unlikely to spur success values into the team. Conversely, a mere junior member in a group who exhibits leadership qualities is more likely to inspire a good influence at that moment.

One is considered emotionally intelligent when they can promptly identify what they feel, interpret, regulate their emotions, understand their impact on others, and manage others' emotions. Pay attention to the following aspects and note how you will develop your emotional intelligence and communications.

Self-Awareness

You need to be able to accurately recognize your emotions, strengths, weaknesses, and actions. Further, understand how they affect the people around you. Regardless of what causes you to feel certain emotions, it is important to know how each emotion affects your thoughts and what actions the thoughts lead you into. Evaluate the effective outcome of the would-be actions and see if it would positively or negatively impact the extent and if necessary.

Keep track of past events that trigger disruptive emotions in you. Get feedback on how others perceived you under the circumstances and focus on deploying your helpful reactions henceforth. Observe how people respond to your new behavior and adjust accordingly. This positive consideration of feedback can also help you build a team with people who have virtue in the areas of your struggle.

Self-Regulation

Beyond being aware of your emotions and impulses, make an initiative to work toward managing them wisely. Consider situations and show or restrain emotions based on what is necessary. For instance, rather than shout at colleagues due to stressful schedules, choose to delegate some of your duties to reduce your workload. Negative emotions are generally overwhelming. Manage and reduce any negative thought that comes to mind.

Where you are in the wrong, do not blame but take responsibility for your mistakes. It will reduce the feeling of guilt, and others will begin to respect you on that account. However, heated a matter gets, try to respond with calm. You communicate more effectively that way, spreading a better feeling to the team. If need calls for it, try to do controlled breathing. Evaluate the situation with objectivity and in a variety of ways so you do not get provoked easily.

Mind your vocabulary. Focus on becoming a stronger communicator. Use precise words to describe deficiencies and work to address them. Pinpoint what wrong is going on and fix exactly that. This will help you avoid stewing upon it and magnifying its effects.

Self-regulation will help you adapt to change more evenly, react rationally, and consequently earn others' respect and trust. Too, practice mindfulness, and you will realize your perspective change for the better.

Empathy

Work at identifying and understanding other people's emotions. Imagine yourself in another's situation and try to capture the same emotions as they would feel. Learn how to read people's feelings from their verbal and non-verbal cues. Notice how far sheer desperation or excitement can lead people and realize how much it will or must have cost them to come out of it well.

Practice listening without interrupting. Learn to observe and gauge people's feelings. When they have low or negative emotions, do not ignore them. Address them. Take time to understand personalities and surrounding circumstances. For instance, socially anxious people need your empathy first. Learn, too, to always keep your body language open with a friendly tonal voice to show your social acceptance for them.

Empathy helps you to respond to concerns genuinely. It ignites compassion and fosters your readiness to help others. It shows you care and helps you deliver feedback. It enhances the bonding and productivity of team-workers. It is not that empathetic statements permit irresponsible behavior, but rather remind us that everyone has their own issues.

Motivation

Emotional intelligence blends with the right choices in what you do in life. Strive always to enjoy what you do and keep striving towards your goals without too importantly considering money or status. Always remember why you do what you do and have the bigger picture in mind at all times. Know what causes you anxiety and strive to have less of it in life. Set new targets and remain positive and optimistic. When facing difficult moments of challenge or setback, try and find one positive factor about them and work by that. Take time to explain to others why they are valuable, no matter the circumstances. It provides and upholds in them a sense of purpose.

Motivation helps reduce procrastination, foster self-confidence, conquer setbacks, and to keep focused on the goals. Motivation will help you bounce back from adversity into your path of success. You will ask positive questions about challenges and draw from them lessons that will strengthen your muscles of hope and positivity, spreading it to the team instantly.

Social Skills

If you turn out to be emotionally intelligent, you will first manifest it by effectively managing your relationships to realize mutual benefits— work at developing your communication skills and listening to feedback with an even mind. Provide praise where necessary, and provide constructive feedback at all times. Strive to be a team player regardless of status or regard.

Listen to others and show empathy. Aim to create and maintain personal relationships with individuals rather than just groups. When conflicts arise, resolve them by accumulating the parties' views and lobbying for compromise, where necessary, for everyone's good.

Social skills are necessary for you to build rapport with people and earn their respect and loyalty. In circumstances where the best decision is unpopular, social skills help you earn people's trust nonetheless. Interaction and identity with individuals can inform how their abilities can be blended for better productivity. Being a sociable person makes others feel comfortable sharing their ideas and concerns with you.

Composure

Composure describes the total personality that you present yourself to be in the face of adversity or crisis. It is your signature of reaffirmation that says, despite how clumsy things may seem midway, the very outcome of your endeavors is already established. It does not depend on the moment to moment confusions that may arise. Composure is when a clearer picture of tomorrow is cast in the dull circumstances of the current moment to make certain the way through.

Leaders need to see adversity from a lens of opportunity too. What presents in the course of another needs to be worked out or worked at. It could be a necessary factor by itself or a pointer to another, and it must not be feared or ignored. Crises result where composure misses. When people sense leadership naivety and unpreparedness, they feel unsafe and insecure and withdraw their leadership trust. Hence leaders must be composed to show poise and control if they lead the team through tough times.

Get Emotions out of the Way

Train yourself to go beyond emotions when you want to solve problems of any sort. Think about what you have to do and dwell on that, and the emotions will subside. Do not be dramatic. Do not yell at colleagues or get overly animated, gesturing at them. Control your emotions and let your body language respond similarly. This will help you to remain objective through the resolution process.

Have a strong will, and use that to keep yourself composed as you handle issues at hand. You are needed to show concern and care so that all hope for the goals is not lost under the prevailing situations.

Do Not Go Personal

Things do not always play out logically. For instance, company-politics and many other dynamics can influence the ongoing processes and pose challenges. It's a collective responsibility, and everybody is involved. You do not need to justify your thoughts and actions of how this could have been avoided. Focus on staying committed to solving the problem and returning systems to normalcy. That is all that is needed for you.

Take control and show that you are doing it well so that you have the support of everyone. Do not get every issue too close to the heart. Do not allow external noise and politics to rule over your thinking and decision-making capability.

Be Optimistic

Keep a positive attitude. You can afford a narrative that gives inspiration and hope. Have the resolve to get things together and better, and stay reminded of your leadership expertise, experience, and role. Show strength, smile, and show your sense of compassion.

Set the right pace and tone. Positive-mindedness gets to work by itself to begin neutralizing chaos, so you follow on to set the right course of correction and advancement. As you do this, focus on harnessing everyone's positive values and setting the correct momentum for everyone's good.

Be Bold

Act beyond fear. Be assertive but not controlling on the team: project confidence and cool and calm personality. Remind yourself and everyone that it is not the crisis that hurts but the outcome that will benefit. So be ready and do not show fear in the face of it.

It is impossible to act rationally under the attack of fear. Courage expands your mind and keeps you focused on the way and how you want to come out of it strongly. Rather than expecting the worst to happen, analyze the current situation, and get in action to manage and resolve it at the earliest opportunity.

Respond Decisively

Do not show doubt. You do not need to know the answer right away to do this. Decide how you want to come out. Know that you have the required means and abilities. Challenges do not come to stop course but to spur commitment and determination. It is not the relative easiness you expect but the resolve to set things right, and that's what must be done at all other expenses.

Speak with conviction, exude your confidence, and show authority. When everyone knows the way, they quickly shift their focus that way. And the sooner they know it and do that, the better for all.

Chapter 10: Body Language Tips

Our body language says more than words or text ever could. It's all that the world needs to see to form an opinion of you. But sadly, we are so poor at body language that we end up giving our insecurities away. Having the right body language indicates self-confidence, and people will always react positively toward a confident person. Self-confidence is critical for communicating effectively. The following are some of the things you might want to do for the sake of your body language.

Smile more often

When you put that smile on your face, you send the message to your brain that you are having a pleasant moment, and the brain, in turn, makes you feel genuinely happy. It doesn't matter what you are going through, but a smile is an instant mood-booster. When you give out information with a smile on your face, people will likely believe you and cooperate with you. This is because people are naturally attracted to people that demonstrate positivity. A smile is the biggest communicator of positive energy. Thus, putting on a smile sends out the message that you have a positive mindset, and people are drawn to you. If you are not used to smiling, it can be a bit challenging to start. You only have to practice regularly, say, every morning, until it becomes second nature.

Keep an erect posture.

Nothing gives away your confidence levels more than your posture. If you are slouching, it means that you are low in confidence. And if you stand upright, it means that you have healthy self-confidence. Assuming a poor posture might send out the wrong signal and cause your audience to tune out. Having an erect posture is primarily about shifting your weight to the balls of your feet, keeping your feet slightly apart, holding your arms by the sides of your torso, and standing straight with shoulders held back. Research shows that assuming the right posture leads to an increase in energy levels, as well as lung capacity, and thus your voice comes out firmer, and you appear confident in your abilities.

Give strong handshakes

Obviously, not all communication opportunities will require that you meet people, let alone shake their hands. But if you intend to share information with a tight circle in the workplace, you may have to approach them physically. One of the most important things to keep in mind is to have a strong handshake. Nothing says "low energy" or "low confidence" more than a limp handshake. But you want people to think of you as a confident person so that they can respect your time and contribution. Giving a strong handshake doesn't mean that you have to try to be macho. You should establish eye contact and smile while shaking their hand.

Improve your fashion sense

They say, "Never judge a book by its cover," but that doesn't apply to us humans, for we most certainly judge people by their looks. If someone is poorly dressed, we form a low opinion of them, and if someone is dressed to impress, we think of the high status. Having a fashion sense isn't necessarily about wearing the latest clothes. It's about being aware of the clothes that compliment your body type and dressing for an event. Generally, impressive clothes are nicely tailored and fitting. Sometimes it's okay to stretch the limits, but then it matters how you handle yourself: always keep your head high. Appear comfortable in whatever you are wearing by having a smile ready.

Break the habit of fidgeting

If you have a fidgeting habit, people will think that you are not sure of your abilities. Splaying your fingers, playing with your hair, and biting your nails indicate that you are trying to suppress your shock and anxiety. Fidgeting is a distraction, for it takes the attention away from the actual conversation. If you realize that you fidget a lot while speaking, there are many things you could to fight away this habit:

1. Speak with your hands: as you speak, try to make subtle motions with your hands, and you won't have to fidget anymore.

2. Fold or clasp your hands: you may also fold your hands and hold them against your body. Or clasp your hands together every time you

are speaking. Remind yourself constantly to undertake this exercise until the habit sticks.

3. Take heavy breaths: obviously, anxiety is the major trigger behind fidgeting. So, how about treating the root cause? Taking deep breaths has long been shown to be an effective method of fighting away anxiety. It calms you down, helping you stop fidgeting.

Establish eye contact

Learn to look at people directly in their eyes. It means that you are both sincere and confident. It also increases your intimacy, causing your message to hit home. If you are not used to looking people in the eyes, it can be pretty challenging at first, but it should come naturally with constant practice. If you are uncomfortable looking at another person's eyeballs, you can just look at the area between their eyes. But then don't become a creep or try to establish dominance. Look away from time to time, and do it slowly. Establishing eye contact also makes you appear more charismatic.

Take up space

Some people have this hideous habit of shrinking themselves when they are in the spotlight. But rarely anyone takes them seriously because they look ridiculous. To be taken seriously, you must project competence, which is still confidence, and one of the ways of doing that is taking up space. So, spread out your hands, stand tall, put your shoulders at ease, and from time to time, adjust and readjust your limbs. It sends out the message that you are unafraid. But more importantly, it makes people comfortable and causes them to treat you respectfully, which means they are bound to listen actively.

Nod when someone else is speaking

we said, communication is two-way. You have to be willing to listen actively just as much as you are willing to speak. One of the methods of demonstrating active listening is through constant nods. By nodding regularly while the other person speaks, it is an indication that you are super attentive, which is a great encouragement to the speaker. But then, in as much as nodding is cool, please don't overdo it. Know when to stop.

Lean subtly

If the speaker delves into something that really piques your interest, you might want to lean forward slightly. But be sure not to lean in too much lest you appear desperate for approval. If you want to appear cool, you can always lean back slightly and give the occasional nod.

Mirror their actions

Psychology teaches us that when we are greatly impressed by someone, we tend to mirror their actions, albeit subconsciously. If you find the speaker interesting, you don't have to wait for your subconscious mind to catch up. You may very well begin to mirror the actions of the other person. If they lean in, then do so, and if they put their hands on their thighs, wait for a moment, and then follow suit. It strengthens your ties with the speaker and causes them to give their all.

Use the right tone.

Your voice is an excellent indicator of your confidence and energy levels. A weak voice points to someone with low self-esteem, and a strong voice indicates high confidence. There are people with small voices and high superior confidence levels, but those are an exception. To sound great, you don't particularly have to thunder or shout yourself hoarse, but reserve the right tone for everything you say. For instance, if you are talking about something fun, use an upbeat voice, and if you are talking about a regretful or sad event, use a calm tone.

Appear focused

You could be having a wonderful posture and appear not intimidated at all, but then have a wandering mind, which spoils it all. Ensure that you are not throwing your eyes to every corner every few seconds. It can actually make people wary. Like, what are you up to? To seem focused, ensure that your eyes are fixed at the speaker or your face is at least facing their direction. Your facial expression should reflect what the speaker is talking about. For instance, if he's trudging his way through a complex concept, you should appear thoughtful, and if he's telling a joke, you should have a light facial expression, as if ready to laugh out at the punch line.

Don't invade other people's space

When you are talking to people, there are some simple rules that you can easily forget. For instance, you can forget to stay within your boundaries and decide to encroach on other people's space. It is a bit creepy when you come too close to another person. So always ensure that there's a healthy space between you and the other people (or person)

Chapter 11: Practice Active Listening

We go through countless meetings in our work weekly. The purpose of those of these meetings is obviously to pass some message across. But the big question is whether or not this message actually reaches its intended audience. It takes active listening to capture the message just as it was intended. Thus there are no misunderstandings and no potential conflict. Here are some of the methods of engaging in active listening:

Face the speaker

You can hardly be an active listener when you are facing away. You have to look at the speaker directly so that you can take in every word and nuance. There are very many nonverbal messages that a speaker sends out, and unless your eyes are on them, you will miss out. Ensure that you look at the speaker in the eyes. But be careful that you don't overdo it. Excessive eye contact can seem intimidating. Establishing eye contact makes sure that you get the whole message and also makes the speaker feel appreciated. Nothing would heartbreak a speaker faster than talking to people who were looking elsewhere but him.

Assume an erect posture

First off, your posture says a lot about you. If you have a poor posture, then it means you are low in confidence, and vice versa is true. An erect posture makes it easy for you to listen actively, for your eyes can now face forward. Avoid crossing arms over your chest or locking your legs. It is a gesture that signifies that you don't want to be disturbed, which is an unfriendly thing to do in a public place. To show the speaker that you are indeed following their every word, you might want to lean in forward slightly or tilt your head a bit as you support it with a palm. Apart from boosting your self-confidence and helping you practice active listening, an erect posture is beneficial for health purposes. It will help with back problems and also boost blood flow.

Never interrupt

Interrupting the speaker is virtually the rudest thing you can do. It shows that you have no time for what they are saying or that you are more important than everybody else, assuming other people are listening. Interrupting the speaker might upset their train of thought and thus ruin their message. You want to ensure that you are cooperating with the speaker and giving them respect. Some issues might be too pressing, and you feel as though you can't wait to raise them. The appropriate way of raising a concern is to note all the issues and then wait for the speaker to be done. This shows that you respect them, and you are more likely to have a great relationship with them.

Avoid jumping to conclusions or judging

People frustrate their efforts of listening actively by constantly jumping to conclusions. This habit can lead to miscommunication and give rise to potential conflict. Ensure that you listen to the speaker until they are done. Jumping to conclusions indicates a lack of patience as well as immaturity on the part of the listener. Equally as bad is the habit of judging others. A speaker might decide to tell a story that touches on their lives, but the listener might decide to start weighing the story in morality scales, trying to determine the speaker's moral conscience. This habit not only takes away from an individual's capacity to practice active listening but also reduces them into a quasi-morality preacher.

Avoid preparing a counter-attack

Some people cannot listen actively because they don't listen to understand, but they listen to give a response merely. For such people, communication is like a sport whereby the winner takes it all, and they want to be the winner and revel in that glory. When you plan to launch a counter-attack as soon as the speaker is done, you didn't have sufficient concentration when the speaker was talking. Chances are you didn't get the whole facts, or you heard them in a skewed manner, thus opening up gaps for conflict. Active listening is about being attentive until the speaker is done. Then you can start to say whatever is on your mind.

Encourage the speaker

Nothing bothers a speaker more than having to talk to someone or a totally unreceptive group. It makes the speaker lose morale and stop putting enough effort into passing their message across. There are many things you can do to encourage the speaker. Some of these things include:

1. Nodding: this is a classic way of showing the speaker that you are on the same page as them. From time to time, and when you lock eyes, give them a slight nod. But you want to be sure that you are economical with the nods lest it appears as though you are trying too hard to impress the speaker.

2. Smiling: this is a way of showing the speaker friendliness. It makes them comfortable. Think about how you'd feel if you started speaking with someone and a group, and then they wore a hostile face? You'd feel unwelcome. But if they had a smile, you'd feel welcome. So, learn to smile regularly at the speaker as it shows him that you are their friend, and it inspires them to keep on.

3. Say "Yes" or "Uh-uh" and other affirming sounds: mouthing off such sounds makes the speaker proud of himself for attracting people's attention, and more importantly, their full engagement.

4. Don't look at the watch every thirty seconds: we tend to frantically look at our watches when we are stuck at a place and can't seem to wait to leave. When the speaker realizes that people are looking at their watches quite frequently, they can assume that they are boring, which

hurts their feelings. It is enough to look at the watch just once and keep reminding yourself not to look again, for it's too soon.

5. Avoid fidgeting: why would you fidget? It's the speaker doing the talking, not you. Does your fidgeting stem from your nervous energy? But why is that? On the part of the speaker, such behavior is as much disturbing as it is discouraging.

Don't offer solutions unless asked to

If a colleague comes up to you and sobs about their challenges, your main function should be holding them steady and listening to them keenly. It would help if you did not attempt to say, "Oh, do this and that -" The rules of active listening demand that you only give guidance and solutions upon request. When you start giving away unsolicited advice, you ignore the wishes of the imagined victim. If you stop wasting time trying to come up with a solution for the speaker's numerous troubles, you would have sufficient time to listen to actually what's being said, understanding the message, regardless of its pain.

Be focused

Another critical facet of active listening is staying focused throughout. Both external and internal, many things might try to grab your attention, but shun them off and stick to listening. Don't expend your mental resources fighting automatic thoughts (the thoughts that seem to overpower your will) but take on the role of the observer, for eventually, these thoughts will fade away. When you are focused on what the speaker is saying, you have a decent chance of hearing the entire message as was intended. This means communication has been carried out flawlessly.

Be curious and creative

When you practice active listening, you are bound to accurately capture the message instead of the person who's distracted or allowed himself to be distracted. But then, if you are the curious type or the creative type, you should see more than one perspective to whatever the speaker says, and thus, you should have a question. Such curious behavior goes a long way in starting and cementing ties between the two parties.

Be open-minded

This green orange – hung in space – whose name is Earth is quite large. In it, their lives all manner of people and creatures. Human beings are different. There is so much variety like you wouldn't believe. For that reason, it would be unfair for any culture or distinct group to declare themselves as more worthy than any other culture or group. Thus, when you are listening to a speaker, you should have an open mind. Since you are probably unfamiliar with their background, you might not be aware of their deep convictions and philosophies, so keep an open mind and accept whatever they say as long as it is within boundaries of respect. Actually, this attitude is great for creativity. It helps you have a multifaceted conception of ideas and things.

Chapter 12: Public Speaking

Speaking to listeners might be fun and thrilling. But, lack of research or not defining the presentation's objectives and its spectators may make even the best-intended appearance a complete tragedy. Public communication skills are important both in an individual's life and in their occupation. Even if someone does not frequently engage in public talking, increasing skills in this region will increase somebody's confidence and lessen nervousness about situations they might be called upon to talk in public. Even people who live with social nervousness disorder might become self-assured speakers, with proficiency development and nervousness management.

Structure of the Presentation

Once the speaker has determined their presentation's purpose and general goal and the listeners, it is time to structure it. The speaker shall need to start this procedure by determining the duration of the appearance.

In this part, the speaker should offer a synopsis of their presentation or a short précis of the speech, elucidating why the speaker covers this subject and what they hope to achieve.

The presentation's opening and the staging's finale are the most vital parts and must have the strongest consequence.

Organize the Room

If possible, the speaker should visit the area to make a public speech in advance. Decide how the audience will sit and decide how the illustration aids that are chosen will appear. Reflect on lighting, room, even the hotness of the room. Think about inserting notebooks and pencils at each chair if members want to take notes. The speaker may also desire to have glasses at every seat with a few water jugs if the presentation will take long. If the speaker does this, they should make sure they permit time for toilet breaks.

While the speaker does not need to remember the entire presentation, they should familiarize themselves with it through many practice runs.

Prepare the presentation in full as frequently as the speaker can before giving it to listeners. The more the speaker practice, the more positive they will be, and the more confident they will seem to the listeners. If the speaker knows their topic and has sufficiently prepared, they will convey their message. When in suspicion or worried, the speaker should stay focused on their point. Express the thoughts to the topic at hand. The addressees have come to hear the presentation, and the speaker will thrive.

Preparation Is Vital

The speaker wants their speech to run, which could not occur if they do not arrange for it. That is not a simple goal, however, and it might be done. The speaker should start by setting aside the date and assemble the piece. They should move on by noting down points they want to put across to the audience. Then organize them rationally, so they flow logically from one to the following. After this, the speaker might mix in something more to clutch the audience's concentration.

Know the Audience

At this point, the speaker knows what to speak about. However, putting it across to the audience is another narrative. First, the speaker needs to recognize who shall be listening when they speak. To state it differently, the speaker should know their audience. Also, they should find ways to get familiar with the listeners. Aspire to be friendly with them.

Consequently, the speaker must dig up their weirdness, desires, aches, and preference peeves. Be conscious of the age bracket of the listeners. Demographics are an essential aspect of discovering the audience. The speaker does not need a proper survey to get this information. The speaker should interact with the audience in the first few minutes of the speech.

Get Satisfied with the Surroundings

The capacity of the location is directly proportional to the speaker's gestures and actions. Big places need huge gestures and extensive movements. Little spaces require the reverse. In a big hall, the speaker needs to plan to have large hand signals and body movements, or else the speaker falls short of engaging the listeners. Suppose the setting is as small as a school classroom, correct consequently. In a tiny space, the speaker rolling their eyes will grasp people's attention. In such a situation, even a half-smile might emphasize a point.

If the speaker checks the speaking site first, they also determine whether they will have the sovereignty to stroll to and fro. Or they will be restricted in a tiny location, like behind a platform. These little details are essentially not tiny at all, and if the speaker thinks systematically about them, they will make all the variation in the speaking engagement.

The Speaker's Appearance

The speaker must make sure they are groomed and looking good in their favorite attire. When the speaker looks great, they feel great too. On the other hand, if the speaker prefers an informal appearance and is suitable for the event, they should go for that non-formal appearance. It will make the speaker feel happier and more appealing to equally casual listeners. Audiences at first judge them based on appearance, so the speaker should make an additional effort to dress to command admiration and self-assurance.

Practice

When the speaker is on the stage, their speech depends on how well they practiced. If the speaker messes up, the listeners shall remember him or her for that. That is a sufficient basis to practice and go on practicing. The speaker should record a video of them practicing the speech and revise their strengths and limitations.

When the speaker records their speech, they will also detect whether they speak too slow or too fast. Consequently, they should adjust their talking pace so their audience shall get the most of the presentation. Analysis of the speech on video is a way to verify if the speaker can talk in monotone. If the speaker does, they should make a point to contrast their tone.

Confidence develops from picking a topic the speaker likes and studying it well. Friendliness may be conveyed purely by smiling at the listeners. Eagerness and energy shall logically follow when the speaker enjoys the topic and are well equipped. If the speaker feels that their stage presence is missing, they should watch clips of speakers whom they respect.

Voice Control

The voice of an individual is the most significant tool they will utilize as a public speaker. The speaker should develop the quality of their voice through diaphragmatic inhalation. This is how proficient musicians inhale. It helps make their vocal sound tremendous and allows them to hold notes extensively after most individuals could be out of breath. By doing so, the speaker reduces feelings of breathlessness triggered by speech nervousness.

Body Language

The speaker should consider their body language and the point that it puts across. An individual should Practice standing with a comfortable upright pose. Place the arms at the sides or clinched in front of the speaker unless they make a signal to highlight a point. Also, the speaker should become conscious of their facial expressions, as well. This implies that they must match the message they are delivering. If the presenter is giving a cheerful speech, they should try to have a calm and pleasant look on their face.

Delivery

When it comes to good public talking, delivery is paramount. Even if the speaker has a good voice and excellent body language, their message shall get lost if they cannot easily follow what the speaker says.

Audience Relationships

Excellent public speakers are in connection with their listeners. Public talking is more than appearing in front of a crowd and chatting. The speaker should acknowledge the listeners right away and start talking as soon as the audience is settled. This aids in making the presenter appear more like a real speaker and keeps an informal pitch. If the presenter needs to set up the apparatus, they should converse with the audience at the same time to maintain their attention.

On the other hand, the presenter must make eye contact and observe for communication from the listeners. Smiles are an excellent indicator; confused looks might mean that the speaker needs to correct what they are doing. But, if the speaker lives with social nervousness, they should be cautious not to focus too much on downbeat faces. It might be that some people are having an awful day, and the expressions have nothing to do with what the speaker is saying. A fine rule of thumb is to locate a welcoming face at the start of the speech. If that individual appears to be bemused or fed up, that is when the speaker knows it is time to tackle issues with their public talking.

Visual Aids

The speaker should consider the use of visual material. Projectors, video apparatuses, and computers must be tested out earlier to ensure they are working properly and that the speaker knows how to use them.

The presenter should make sure they do not revise too much information onto any particular illustration. A fine rule to apply is to keep every illustration to six lines. The presenter should make sure any sort of graphics is big enough. This enables the audience to see it plainly. The colors applied should be simple to enable good viewing by the audience.

Outlay should be evidently marked and arrange in order earlier. Flip charts must be arranged in advance as well. When applied during the speech, the speaker should make the print big enough for all members to see. When the speaker is applying these diverse visuals, they should not turn the back to the listeners. The visual aids should be positioned well, so the presenter may observe the visuals while looking at the audience.

Influential Speech

When selecting a topic for their influential speech, it is vital to reflect on the audience's composition. Because influential speeches are planned to influence or strengthen an audience's judgment or behaviors, speakers ought to think about what and how the listeners think and believe. The audience may be undecided about the topic or powerfully opposed, in strong conformity, or somewhere along the continuum. In convincing speeches, it counts where they fall on this scale. For example, if the speaker wants to disagree that abortion must be illegal, and the audience is made up of pro-life activists, the speech may seem like the presenter is preaching to a singing group.

Since those listeners no longer desire to be convinced. But, the speaker may find themselves in states that allow them to plea to a receptive audience. For instance, parents are commonly concerned about keeping their children protected.

Chapter 13: Speech Delivery

The Moment of Truth

The actual delivery of the speech is your moment to shine. For some, this part is the most stressful part of delivering a speech.

This is the real thing. After making your draft and practicing speaking a couple of times, this is the moment of truth.

It is most important to keep your calm and focus on what you are about to do in this part.

Effective Delivery

To deliver your speech effectively, you need to look natural in front of your audience. Avoid being too stiff or being too shaky. For you to be more natural and confident, you must:

1. Act Normal

It would help if you kept in mind that your speech is like any other normal conversation you can have with any other normal person.

A speech is only a little different because many people are listening to you all simultaneously.

However, you don't have to be nervous about this. Just think of everyone as your friend. Smile and be confident. If you are well prepared, there is nothing to be nervous about.

You can just imagine everyone in their underwear. If this old trick works for you, then go for it. Don't try to act it out. Try to keep everything as normal as you can.

2. be enthusiastic

Even if you are the one speaking, you need to show some enthusiasm over your topic.

If your listeners see that you are excited about speaking, then they might be excited too.

This will spark some interest in your audience and help you keep their attention for a longer time.

3. be confident

Don't think too much about how you look, instead focus on what you are saying.

Don't be too conscious of yourself in front of your audience. It will only increase your nervousness.

If you are not confident yourself, how will your audience have confidence in you and what you say?

4. Maintain Proper Contact

When speaking, do not avoid the audience. What you should do is engage with them. Remember to maintain eye contact with everyone.

Shift your focus from one person to another to see if everybody is listening. Maintaining your focus on only one person may cause him or her to be uncomfortable.

However, if you just stare into blank space, your audience may not find your speech exciting or interesting. Also, try to use a friendly tone of voice. Don't talk too loud or shout.

You just need your voice to be heard clearly. You may raise your voice when pointing out a fact or an important idea.

But throughout your speech, you should try to talk in a calm and friendly manner. Also, don't forget to smile.

Remember to smile when you can and smile at the audience. If possible, put yourself in a place near your audience. This will create familiarity and comfortable air around you.

Methods of Delivery

You can deliver your speech in many ways. As a speaker, you need to be familiar with the different methods of speaking.

But soon enough, you can try to develop your own style and approach to speaking. Here are the most common types of delivering a speech.

1. Manuscript

Speaking with a manuscript is the easiest way to do a public speech. You just need to read a prepared speech and hope that everything goes well. Most people do this type of delivery.

However, this restricts you from maintaining eye contact with your audience, which is a must.

You can still try to have brief eye contact as you read, but much of your focus is on the paper you are reading.

This also restricts you from moving your body to show a point or portray conviction.

As much of your attention is on the paper, you are reading, and you don't have much freedom to move and express yourself.

This type of delivery, although easy, maybe boring for the audience. Soon enough, their attention will drift away from you, and you will have a hard time getting it back.

However, there are ways where you can still deliver an effective speech while reading a manuscript.

With enough experience and practice, you can speak in front of an audience without them getting bored, even while reading from a manuscript.

If you are about to read your speech, here are a few things you need to do:

Use presentation aids to keep the attention of your audience.

Take some time to read the whole speech and be familiar with it. This will help you avoid stuttering and making mistakes.

It will also allow you to have some eye contact with your listeners.

Use a font style that you are familiar with, and try to put large spaces between your manuscript lines. This will allow you to read it with ease and avoid misunderstanding words or phrases.

2. Memory

Delivering your speech from memory is a hard thing to do. First of all, if your speech is long, it would be hard to memorize it all.

Second, sometimes, when doing the actual speech, you may forget something important, and you end up confusing your audience.

However, delivering a speech from your memory may make you appear more professional.

If you can do it properly, you took the time to make your speech and know the important details you need to discuss.

Sometimes, you really can't help but forget something, so it is important to outline.

If you have memorized your speech, you can bring this outline with you while you talk. Sure, it does not contain your whole speech, but it has the key points and ideas you want to talk about.

But if you are still a bit unsure, you can bring with you your manuscript. Just take glances when you forget something.

There are still instances when memorized speeches are used. Speeches like this are common in toasts and introductions, where you only need to say a few short sentences.

Delivering a speech from memory has a few advantages:

You can maintain eye contact with your audience if you deliver your speech from memory and analyze how they think or react to your speech.

Maintaining eye contact is important for you to keep a certain bond or connection with your audience.

You can move around freely. Without a piece of paper consuming your focus, you now move around and interact with your audience. You can go around the stage and move your limbs freely. This will help you convey information more effectively.

You can express yourself more and vary the tone of your voice. You can smile, frown, or laugh when you have the most of your focus on your audience. Just like having the freedom of movement, this will also allow you to express your message more effectively.

3. Impromptu

Impromptu speaking is when you are not prepared to give a speech, which means you need to improvise.

This can happen in many places, especially in celebrations, where you will be asked to do a little speech for someone.

This can also happen in school when your professor asks you to summarize a lesson from your book.

When speaking impromptu, you can be unprepared, but do not panic. There things that you can do to ensure a good outcome for your speech.

Take a deep breath and focus on the situation. If you can, try to do a little bit of research first, but if you can't, just focus on what you know about the topic and what you would really want to say to your audience.

On a piece of paper, write down the key idea, phrases, or topics you would want to discuss. If you can, arrange them into a neat order and use a simple outline.

Stay focused on your topic. Do not wander off and try to talk about other things, get straight to the point, and avoid too many words.

Don't speak too fast because your audience may not understand you. Instead, try to appear calm and speak slowly. This will allow you to gather your ideas while speaking.

Chapter 14: Improving Conversation Skills

Sending emails and texts and making calls are all methods of communication. But it is only through conversations that we can connect with other people sincerely. But the problem is that not many of us are really good at making conversation. We fumble through sentences and find ourselves not making any sense, which makes us appear uncharismatic. The following are some tips to help you become better at conversations:

Speak more slowly

It is difficult to make any sense when you speak very fast, yet you lack the mental alertness of what you say. This puts you at risk of making errors and sounding fake. If you try to boost your charisma and conversation skills, start by learning to speak slowly. Besides having the time to think through what you say, speaking slowly makes you seem like a calm and confident person, which is the ultimate projection of confidence. The following are some of the ways to help you master talking slowly:

1. Record yourself: you cannot really know how fast or slow you talk unless you listen to yourself. Thankfully, we live in a technologically advanced period, were recording your voice is

possible. So, record yourself many times as you attempt to speak in a slow and yet charismatic fashion.

2. Gain inspiration from successful "slow" speakers: many world-renowned people have a "slow" speaking style. Learn from them. Watch hours of footage as they get interviewed and get inspired by how they handle themselves.

3. Relax: before you can speak slowly, you need to eliminate anxious thoughts and feel free. Relaxing will help you come off naturally when you start speaking. One of the best ways to relax and calm your nerves is by taking deep breaths.

4. Master pronunciation: one of the factors that make you sound articulate is word pronunciation. If you get that right, you have taken a big step forward. When you master enunciation, you sound not only articulate and natural but also sophisticated.

Look people in the eyes

Wouldn't it be weird to have a conversation with someone who was staring off? You can get away with not looking at the speaker in the eye in a group setting since many people are around anyway. But when you have a conversation with a person, you had better face them and look in their eyes. Establishing eye contact shows that you approve of the other person and are confident in yourself. It makes the environment just right for cultivating close professional ties. If you find yourself embarrassed at looking people in the eyes, that's an indication of underlying issues like shame, and you have to get rid of that.

Notice things that ordinary people wouldn't

Nothing gives a boost to your charisma more than being different yet in an understated fashion. The average person is likely to notice the big, shiny things. But if you are the type of person who notices the little and inconspicuous details, you are way more charismatic. Subtly inspect your environment and bring up the inconspicuous details, to the amazement of the other party. The following tactics can improve your capacity to notice these inconspicuous details:

1. Don't multitask: when you have a conversation with another party, avoid being engaged in other distractions like phone and computer. Focus on the conversation and what's happening around you.

2. be self-aware: your attention is likely to wander off, but you must know when to tune right back. Keep reminding yourself that you are supposed to stay focused.

3. Reduce your information load: don't gobble too much information that you lose track of what's important. Just focus on one thing at a time.

Become great at giving compliments

An average person is always ready to mouth off a thoughtless and cliché complement that won't arouse any excitement. But a charismatic person is skilled at giving compliments. They give unique compliments. To become a great conversationalist, you have to develop your capacity to give compliments by doing the following:

1. Talk about something you find fascinating about the other party

2. Find out which accomplishment of theirs that they are most proud of and then give a compliment touching upon it

3. Cleverly frame your words and say things that aren't obvious

4. Don't compliment every person in just one style. They might think you are a fake person

5. Avoid touching on bodily issues and stick to their triumphs, strengths, and other positive things

6. Draw a barrier; be generous, but don't overdo it, lest you appear desperate to impress

Stir their emotions

If you desire to stay in someone's mind for the longest time possible, then stir their emotions. Let your words rip their hearts and have them cry. This is no invitation to tell lies, but you just have to come up with a way, mostly words and body language, that carry so much weight and that will hit the other party and stir emotions. One story can be told by two narrators and yet elicit different reactions from the audience. The audience might be moved by one narrator and get bored by the other one. So, learn to coordinate your words and body language to stir emotions in the other party. To be charismatic, you have to avoid being boring, which means you have to be a pretty creative person.

Offer unique insights

An average person can watch the news or read the papers and make a cliché observation. You don't want to be that. Instead, you want to be the person that has a multi-faceted approach to issues. You can see insights that other people can't. You can see angles to a story that most people wouldn't discern. And this causes the other party to think of you as an interesting person. To build your charisma, you have to have opinions beyond what the common person would say. Thus, if you start speaking, people will instantly pay attention.

Be a showman

The late Steve Jobs, a co-founder of Apple Inc., was both a tech genius and a marketing genius, which was evident in his showmanship during product launches. Being a showman is all about entertaining people. And guess what? Everyone loves to be entertained. These are some of the things you can do to appear like a true showman:

1. Tell funny stories: it's the easiest way to get people to laugh

2. Make fun of yourself: it will boost your charisma and draw people closer to you. But you have to draw a line because past a certain point. It only amounts to being unfair to yourself

3. Ask questions: try to find out what the other party is all about. This is a major way of finding something to talk about

Have a healthy self-esteem

Not all conversations will turn out as you had expected. Thus, ensure that you have healthy self-esteem to cushion from the roughness of the world. For instance, you might run into a nasty person that not only rejects your opinions and philosophies but also yells out profanities at you. If such a scenario plays out, ensure that you keep your cool. There are few things on Earth worth fighting over, but a mere difference of opinion isn't one of them.

Be open

This does not mean that you should disclose every little piece of information about yourself, but you should certainly allow the other party to know you. This is a basic step in connecting with other human beings. We are most comfortable around people that we know of at a much deeper level.

Observe basic manners

Nothing would injure your reputation more than being a person of poor manners. Whatever you do or say, always remember that people are watching. There are some codes of conduct required only among certain classes, but then there are basic manners, and these cut across all the classes. They include:

1. Saying, "Please."

2. Saying "thank you."

3. Apologizing

4. Keeping a pleasant attitude as opposed to hostility

5. Saying "excuse me" when you need someone's attention

Observing basic manners is required of you, not just for conversational purposes, but also to coexist harmoniously with other people. The benefits of observing basic manners include:

1. Elimination of conflict: respect is promoted, and the need to fight is done away with

2. It promotes cooperation: basic manners ensure that people have cooperation and can decide on a way forward, and if not, they can agree to disagree

3. It promotes connections: at the end of the day, humans are social creatures, and we rely on our interdependence to make progress

Chapter 15: Being Charismatic

Ever want to be the person that enters a room, and everyone's face lights up, and they seem eager to hear from you? That's the basic definition of a charismatic person. They are great at charming people. Thankfully, being charismatic is not an inborn trait but merely a skill. This means anyone can develop a charismatic personality as long as they choose to invest in themselves. The following tips help build a charming personality:

Fight off your nervousness

If you watch any person you consider charismatic, you will notice that they have no nervous energy. Everything appears to flow smoothly for them. Before you take up a speaking opportunity, ensure that you are in a relaxed state of mind. Some of the things you might do to fight off your nervousness include:

1. Deep breathing: take slow deep breaths to calm your mind.

2. Pep talk: ever seen how a coach talks to his team to empower them? Yes, you can do that to yourself as well. Get in the habit of giving yourself a pep talk and telling yourself that you can be a charming person and draw people to you.

3. Exercise: go and perform some physically straining exercises to release endorphins in your brain that light up your mood.

Listen actively

Charismatic people are not only good at speaking but also listening. This is a skill that many of us lack. Active listening is about paying full attention to the person who's speaking. Most of us tend to be distracted and thus stopping ourselves from getting the full message. The following tips would improve an individual's capability to listen actively:

1. Face the speaker: ensure that your eyes are fixed on the speaker.
2. Be relaxed: in as much as you want to be attentive, be relaxed too.
3. Have an open mind: understand that people come from different backgrounds, and they may not share the same opinions or philosophies as you. As long as they are not saying or doing outrageous stuff, then keep an open mind.
4. Call on your imagination: while the speaker goes on, create images in your mind to capture what's going on.
5. Don't interrupt: one thing about charismatic people is that they are patient. If they have a concern, they will wait until the time is right to raise that concern.

Ensure that you sound relatable

You have to come across as someone that exists in the same space as them, not a galaxy-trotting alien. Your experiences should be relatable. The following are some tips to make you more relatable:

1. Reveal your struggles: no matter who you are, you must be facing, or at least must have faced, some form of struggle. There's nothing wrong with struggling, considering that it forms a huge part of what builds up our character. By revealing some of your struggles, you end up inspiring people to carry on with their lives with an emboldened spirit. But you have to draw a line: don't disclose too much personal stuff.

2. be original: never try to portray yourself as someone that you're not. If you do, people will smell it, and you will look bad. Being original makes the conversation flow seamlessly.

3. Put your fears out there: make people realize that you are no different than them by expressing your fears. They might not be the same fears that they have, but at least it will show them that you don't perceive yourself as some sort of superman.

Center your discussion on what you are passionate about

Don't be the kind of person that blabbers out any random thought. Being charismatic requires you to be calculative. To infect your listeners with charm, you have to be high-energy. And this can be achieved by talking about your passions. You are likely to have a lot of energy when talking about things you are passionate about. It also brings you pretty close to your goal.

Be a giver rather than a taker

One thing about charismatic people is that they have an abundance mindset. They give, give, give, give, and then take. People are drawn to them because of their evident selflessness. They hope to get answers to their existential problems. Also, realize that being a giver doesn't mean you'll deplete your resources, but you'll actually earn back far more.

Improve your sense of humor

Nothing makes people warm up to you faster than a great sense of humor. To some extent, being humorous is an inborn trait, but you can still develop your capacity to be humorous. There's no science involved. It's basically a mixture of many things, including trends and research. Follow these tips to become more humorous:

1. Watch comedy: you can learn a lot from comedians on telling jokes, particularly land punch lines. However, desist from shouting insults as most commercial comedians do. Also, don't be too dramatic.

2. Look at things from another angle: most humorous people have an eccentric way of looking at things. This forms a huge part of their humor. So, learn to generate more than one idea when processing events or activities.

3. Use simple, descriptive language: you might have an interesting joke but fail to make anyone laugh because of a poor word choice. So, always ensure that you are selecting the right words, which are usually simple and descriptive.

4. Work on your voice: tonal variation is critical in telling jokes, especially if there's more than one character involved.

5. Don't lose yourself: sometimes, you may want to impress others too badly that you end up doing – or saying – something that is so not you. Don't let it get to that point. If the other party is not receptive to our jokes, keep a positive attitude, and move on to other things.

Make people feel important

Not everyone will agree, but yes, everyone is looking for validation. Behind every action of theirs, there's a subtle, and sometimes not-so-subtle, "Hey, look at me!" vibe going on. When you make people feel important, they are likely to drop their guards and be receptive to you. Some of the ways of making people feel important to include:

1. Remember their names
2. Show them that you admire them
3. Appreciate them for what they have done
4. Compliment their tastes
5. Notice anything new about them

Take a sincere interest in others

The keyword is "genuine" because you could easily fake interest, but people can smell fake when they see it. Being genuinely interested in other people will make you seem charismatic. Most people are generally selfish, only interested in their own matters, and it's a welcome break to see someone interested in other people.

Avoid distractions

Once you start engaging another person (or a group), don't succumb to distractions. This means that you stay away from your phone and avoid casting glances on your monitor. Giving other people your full attention will make them see you as a charismatic person.

Have a positive attitude

Charisma and a positive mindset go hand in hand. You cannot have one and lack the other. Having a positive attitude means that you are full of hope. People are drawn to individuals with a positive mindset because they will inspire them. This is how you cultivate a positive attitude:

1. Surround yourself with positive people: whether you are at work or home, stay in the company of positive individuals. Whenever you are feeling low, they will infect you with positive energy.

2. Consume positive media: ensure that you consume content that influences you positively. In this age of the Internet, it is easy to get sucked into negative vices such as watching porn and masturbating, discouraging developing a positive mindset.

3. be kind: extend an olive branch to those who are in need. Studies show that being kind makes us feel great about ourselves. And positive energy wells up, particularly when we are feeling great about ourselves.

Avoid gossiping

If you want to appear charismatic, you have to stay away from idle chat, especially gossiping. Actually, gossip might cause people to shun you. Gossips are responsible for so much pain in society, and people generally tend to stay away from the agents of pain.

Chapter 16: The Art to Make Questions

Why Questioning

We ask questions to:

• Gather information. The information helps us to learn more and add to our knowledge of something, solve problems, make informed and balanced decisions and understand each other clearly and at a deeper level

• Maintain control of a conversation. When you want specific information from a conversation, you become more assertive and ask questions leading the conversation in that direction

• Express our interest in the respondent. We want to find out more about them, and build a rapport with them, or show empathy to them, or just get to know them better

• Seek clarity on points. We want someone to come out clearly on what they are saying so that they are distinctly understood. This helps to reduce misunderstandings and make communication more effective

• Explore the personality of the respondent and what they are experiencing in life. We want to know their beliefs, their ideas and their attitudes, and any circumstances of difficulty that they may be enduring

• Test knowledge. You want to know whether you or the other person is adequately informed about something. Examinations do exactly this

• Spur further thoughts. You want someone to think deeper or differently about something. For instance, 'Why do you think Nairobi is the capital city of Kenya?'

• Include all members, encourage discussion on a particular point, and keep everyone's attention in a group discussion. For instance, asking participants to give more contributions, asking a specific one to speak on the point of discussion, etc.

How Questions Are Asked

For one to ask a question, you perform the following simple steps:

Establish the Purpose of the Question

First, know why you need to ask the question. Evaluate the kind of response you expect. The meaning you want to draw from the response. And what you want to do with what you make of it.

Select the Type of Question

Ask yourself whether the question is relevant to the person or group. Consider if it is the right time and how you want or expect them to respond.

Consider These Factors

Structure

Consider the circumstances under which you are asking the question and structure the question appropriately. For instance, you may need to introduce yourself. Or you may need the background to it. Or you may need to state the reason for the question. Or you may need to ask a few other questions ahead of or afterward.

Establishing the structure helps to run the conversation between the questioner and respondent smoothly.

Silence

The silence between 3 and 5 seconds is a powerful tool, too, by which a question can be delivered. Silence before a question emphasizes the message just delivered. The silence after a question prevents you from asking the next question and tells the respondent that a reply is required. A further silence after the reply has been given tells the respondent that more detail is required.

Participation

In a group scenario, you may want to involve as many participants as possible in the debate. For instance, a question may be redirected from an active participant to a quieter member. Though this doesn't mean the quiet member is forced to speak when they do not want to.

Questioning Methods

Open and Closed Questions

Closed questions are questions that require a single word, very short, or factual answers. The respondent is supposed to respond with definite stances and is not required to give details. If options are provided, they are only a few, or even if they are more, the respondent can only pick a few. Closed questions are best suited for testing one's understanding, concluding a discussion, making a decision, or for frame-setting.

Frame setting asks a question so that the respondents are forced to see the issue with a certain frame of mind. For instance, 'Pleased to meet with the Vice-Chancellor of the institutions?' Closed questions must be avoided when the discussion is in full flow because it can suddenly terminate the conversation. The respondent, feeling uncomfortable to respond to the question in the way you do not expect, might go quiet and result in awkward silence. Most closed questions begin with 'Who…' or 'Which…' or 'Where…' or 'Choose…' etc.

Open questions require long answers. The respondent tells their story in narrating an event, how it occurred, or why it occurred. They are free to speak out their knowledge, opinions, and feelings about something without being restrained or confined. Open questions are used to develop an open conversation, establish more details, and find opinions on issues. Most open questions begin with 'what…' or 'Why…' or 'How…' or 'Describe…' or 'in your…' etc.

Funnel Questions

Funnel questioning is a method that begins with general questions then drills down to more specific points in each. At each level, more and more details are inquired. This method helps the respondent bring more details about something or an event and zoom in on the important details. Begin by asking closed questions, then move on to more open ones as the conversation progresses.

Use this approach when you want to find out more details about a specific point. When you are gaining more interest in someone or increasing their confidence, this is the method to use. See the following:

You: You attended high school?

Respondent: Yes.

You: In which school?

Respondent: Himalayas.

You: Himalayas Boys'.

Respondent: No. Actually, Himalayas Mixed.

You: Oh, I see. So, you took Computer Studies, it was offered in the school even then…, as a subject and that's where you realized you had this passion for computers.

Respondent: Yes.

You scored a good grade in the subject, creating a way for you to join the Macadamia School of Computing and Robotics. Tell us more about that.

Respondent: Blah blah blah…

You: Let's narrow into this Robotics subject. What especially did you do with it to become what you are today?

Respondent: Blah blah blah…

Probing Questions

Probing questions are used to find out more details. You can do this by asking for an example that will help you understand the statement just made. You can also ask for additional information for clarification purposes. You can inquire whether there's proof of what is said and what the proof is. The word 'exactly' is used to make the respondent give as precise detail as possible.

Use this method to gain clarification and ensure you have the whole story and understand it wholly. If you are interviewing a person you think is trying to withhold or alter some details, this is the method you use to extract information.

What exactly was said in the last paragraph?

Leading Questions

You use leading questions when you want to lead the respondents in your thinking direction without forcing them, nor them realizing or trying to resist. You may do that by beginning the question with an assumption, e.g., 'How early do you think he will make there?' This question supposes that he will make it there early. You can also lead by adding a personal appeal to agree at the end, often using a tag question, e.g., 'He will get there early; don't you think so?' The tag question suggests that the respondent agrees that he (subject in the sentence example) will get there early.

You can also phrase it such that the respondent finds it easier to say yes, e.g., 'You would like me to serve you tea instead. Yes?' The respondent is forced to say yes, or otherwise explain himself out, which is more work than they will largely avoid. You can also choose to give two options, both of which make you happy. This method makes you get what you want, but the respondent is left to feel they had no choice to use to stop you. It can also be used to close a deal, e.g., 'Now that all conditions are met, shall we append our signatures?'

However, this method should not be overused or misused because it can be seen as self-serving for you and harming others' interests, telling you to be manipulative and dishonest.

Rhetorical Questions

These are questions that do not require to be answered because they are basically statements phrased as questions. This method is quite pleasantly engaging for the audience. The audience is drawn to think by themselves and agrees with you rather than to be told. It is a good way of getting people to agree with your point of view. Rhetorical questions can be more powerful when used in a string.

Who doesn't want to take their kids to school? And who doesn't like it when their children eventually finish school and graduate with good grades? And when they get employment and come home with that shopping every next month of every year, what better feeling can one get than joy and contentment?

Using Questioning Techniques

The different questioning methods can be used independently or in combination, depending on how you want to lead the conversation. Below, we suggest the situations in which certain questioning methods would apply best.

Learning

Open questions help you to expand your coverage of topics. In contrast, the closed questions will help you ascertain your understanding of the various facts about the topics where your understanding is shallow and probe further to deepen it appropriately.

Relationship Building

Your counterpart is more likely to respond positively when you ask them about what they do or for their opinions. Do so in an affirmative way, and they will open up with more ease. For instance, 'So tell me, what have you come to like best about our offers?' 'Ask open questions and maintain an open dialogue.

Managing and Coaching

Rhetorical and leading questions are best suited in this situation. You make your suggestion using a leading question and ask them to agree with you in rhetorical questions. This combination helps the respondents to reflect and commit to your suggested courses of action.

Avoiding Misunderstanding

When trying to avoid a looming misunderstanding whose consequences can be dire, use the probing technique to establish details of the causes. This method requires you to probe deeper and deeper into why every answer is being given. When the answers begin to make little sense, or the answers' usefulness diminishes, the likely corrective measure becomes obvious. The one advantage of this method is that it prevents hurried jump to conclusions.

Defusing a Heated Situation

Use framed questions to make an angry person see more details about their grievance. This invokes their minds into action and distracts them from their feeling of sadness. It will also provide a window for you to see a practical way of intervening to make them feel better.

Persuading People

Keep asking open questions that will help them see and embrace the reasons behind your point of view. Agreeing along with you, they feel positive to engage in what you ask of them willingly.

So, the art of questioning can be developed. By testing yourself in various situations, you will master the skill and nurture it to full development. It is important to allow your correspondents enough time to think and respond to your questions in the closing remarks. Create a rapport and maintain that relationship throughout the discussion. Secondly, be a skillful thinker and a careful listener to understand what the answers really mean as intended by the corresponded. Finally, your body language and tonal voice will play a significant role in determining the answers you get for the questions asked. Ask right and in the right manner, and you will get the right answers.

Chapter 17: Assertive Communication

For some of us out there, speaking to someone in a casual atmosphere may be easy, while speaking to someone in a more forced social situation may make us more inclined to hide from the world than anything else. There are also instances where we fumble over our words, overact, fidget too much, say inappropriate things, or feel we need to fill the silence by saying something. Or perhaps, it's as simple as being shy or having social anxieties. Learning the basics of communication is only part of your journey to improve your social skills. The other parts are for you to understand what your goals are and for you actually to put them into play.

There are three basic communication areas we'll be going over. These are non-verbal communication, basic social skills, and real-world application. Non-verbal communication normally deals with body language, which accounts for 55% of effective communication. In comparison, the verbal aspect accounts for the other 45% by splitting them into separate categories: the tone of voice and words. Your tone of voice accounts for 38% of effective communication, while the words you and others say are the lowest at only 7%. Now, why do you think that is? Why do you think we pick up on someone's body language and the sound of their voice more than what they're actually saying?

It's because unspoken forms of communication are universal. They go back before we learned how to talk and when we knew what words were. These are the first things we come to understand at a very young age. When a baby laughs, it must mean it thinks something is funny. When a baby cries, we instinctively think something is wrong. When we speak lovingly to a baby, they begin to respond not only to the voice but to the action that follows. In short, you can say this has been programmed into us since a very young age. This is something we have taught ourselves to recognize comfort, safety, and nourishment. As this is the very first thing we learned, we unknowingly take any indication of that safety and comfort from the people around us as we get older. We see gestures before we speak. We hear the tone before we listen to words. We understand the other person's message before we get involved with the conversation. By visually assessing and understanding the tone, you get a notion of how this person may feel.

In addition to these non-verbal aspects, there is listening. Listening is actually a form of communication; however, we'll be focusing on Active Listening. This communication art requires the listener to be engaged in the conversation by having your ears open more so than trying to convey or fill in the silence with words. This is actually very important to those who are trying to connect. They want someone who is going to listen and understand their message. If you're the quiet type already, then you're already there, not because you're silent, but because you know how to listen and observe overall. Staying silent can tremendously work to your advantage at times when used properly.

To help you build a genuine rapport with others, active listening gives you the advantage of understanding your partner or group members more easily. This opens up opportunities to chime in with some nuggets of wisdom after they're done. This shows others that you're willing to listen to what they have to say, relate, and not judge but help if need be. For you, this builds trust between you and whomever you speak with. However, if you're the nervous type and still find yourself struggling with social situations like these, here's some advice about active listening.

Active Listening is where you listen for the sake of understanding, not for replying. Many people only stay silent to build a rebuttal, but if you're trying to get people to like who you are, it's best to understand what they're trying to say instead of spending energy and nerves scrambling for something to say in exchange. You want the others to feel safe around you and open up possibilities to meet up in the future. To be a good listener, don't judge. Let people talk and engage with them in their moments.

As you're listening, take note of how they sound. Do they sound happy? If they do, then perhaps what they're saying is going to lead to something funny? Do they sound disappointed? If they do, then perhaps you should offer some feedback by relating to a similar situation you once experienced? Do they sound irritated? If they do, then perhaps lending some advice to help them see a silver lining will help? Regardless of what you are listening to, always save what you want to say for last. To make sure they're done speaking, just wait for them to fall silent. You can say things like "Well," or "You know what," after you've listened and understood what they were trying to say. As someone meeting others for the first time, don't feel as though you can't say what's on your mind; just remember there are appropriate and inappropriate things that others will either have you liked or ignored.

Let's talk about Body Language again. As mentioned, body language accounts for 55% of effective communication. This is your first step in determining your conversation's direction and even understanding if the other person is engaged or not. This should also be something you're mindful of when speaking to others, too, since you are also part of this conversation and trying to make an impression. A person's body language is based on their personality. For you, you want to use positive body language, not body language that tells others that you're not interested, scared, fidgety, or have anxiety. The non-verbal movements and gestures convey interest, enthusiasm, and positive reactions to what others are saying. If you want to make sure you aren't hurting your chances, try making a checklist of what to look out for.

Chapter 18: Empathy

Empathy is one of the most vital characteristics of being an effective communicator. It is the foundation of all successful personal, professional, and social relationships. Identifying how others around you think and feel, and using this information to make them feel heard and understood, is one of the greatest gifts you can possess. Being empathetic allows you to reach out to people and understand how they feel by placing yourself in their shoes. You understand feelings and emotions from their perspective or experience them exactly as the person feels them. Empathy is the most important secret ingredient for those looking to boost their social skills.

Empathy is not just feeling bad for someone (like sympathy) but, in effect, feeling what they are going through as if you were going through it yourself.

I'll let you in on one of the most potent rapport-building secrets. People who demonstrate a high level of empathy listening to others, keenly tuning in to their emotions, and acknowledging their feelings can instantly build lasting bonds with others. They can communicate more effectively and understand other people's feelings and emotions. They can connect with people at a deeper level to forge more meaningful and lasting bonds. Develop higher empathy by keenly listening to others and tuning in to their verbal and non-verbal communication signals. People do not just communicate through words. They also convey a lot by leaving unspoken through non-verbal cues such as body language, expressions, and voice tone. When you plug into people's non-verbal communication patterns, you can comprehend their message at a subconscious level. This facilitates the process of rapport building and getting people to like and trust you.

Empathy is the cornerstone of emotional intelligence, and being emotionally intelligent allows you not just to identify other people's emotions but also to regulate these emotions for the overall good.

To increase your empathy factor and transform into the ultimate people magnet, place yourself in another person's position and try to understand their situation. Attempt to understand why they do what they do. What is it like to go through a problem they are experiencing? Even if you disagree with them, try to understand where they are coming from (more on pointers for increasing empathy later). Actively imagine the feelings and experiences they are encountering. What can be done to make things easier for them? How can you help them cope with their feelings and emotions without being intrusive? When someone is talking about a highly emotional experience, one tip is to question how you react in the given situation.

At times, people won't directly tell you how they are feeling. However, they'll offer plenty of non-verbal clues that allow you to understand how they feel at a subconscious level. This has been prevalent since primitive times when spoken language wasn't invented. People shared their feelings, thoughts, ideas, and emotions through gestures and sounds. Since primordial times, people have been communicating through non-verbal signals, which have withstood various phases of evolution and language creation as a form of communication. People share a lot through gestures, movements, expressions, posture, walk, voice, etc. Non-verbal communication is more effective than verbal communication, which is why people always insist that they meet 'face to face' when they have something important to convey. It adds a lot of weight to the entire message.

When people do not tell you how they are actually feeling, and you still want to reach out and demonstrate empathy, analyzing people's body language can do the trick. Closely pay attention to read what people leave unspoken, which is evident through their non-verbal signals. Stay intuitive when it comes to latching on to the frequency of others' emotions.

Closely analyze people's facial expressions, eye movements, walk, gestures, leg movements, and posture to determine who they are feeling. Does their body language appear to match what they are speaking? For example, if a person is declaring that they aren't bothered by something but clearly appear preoccupied or fidgety (non-verbal clues such as fluctuating eye contact, tapping fingers or toes, playing with objects, and so on), their actions or non-verbal communication is not in sync with their words or verbal communication. Non-verbal communication can be a straight giveaway when people hold back their stories. One of the most significant signs of an effective communicator is reading what people leave unsaid and matching it against what they say to identify if their verbal communication and non-verbal communication are in sync.

Empathy also involves learning to read between the lines or picking up what people often leave unsaid. Let us look at an example to understand this more effectively. Learning to read between the lines will boost your empathy factor. Say you make a reservation for your family at a posh new eatery in the city. On walking in, you are warmly welcomed and greeted by a dedicated waiter assigned to a table occupied by your family. Then comes the fancy dinner, which is nothing short of a splendid, multi-course dining experience. You are served a lavish, scrumptious, and impeccably presented seven-course meal with all the usual bells and whistles of an upscale dining venue. Before each course is done, the server offers everyone interesting trivia and little-known details about each dish, including its preparation method, ingredients, history, and more, with haunting tunes playing in the background.

After consuming a hearty seven-course meal, you ask for the check. The manager eagerly seeks your feedback since it is a new eatery. He inquires if your family enjoyed the entire 'wine and dine' experience. Your brusque reply is, "The dessert was nice." This disappoints the manager. He doesn't look too happy with your feedback. On the surface, this appears to be a compliment. However, your selection of words reveals something that you've left unsaid. Even without saying it, you have communicated to the manager that the dessert was the only item worth mentioning on the menu or nothing other than the dessert was good. To sum it up, everything else was pretty average.

Did you actually say everything other than the dessert was crap? No right? Yet, by reading between the lines, it is evident that this was what you intended to imply. People convey a lot, not just by what they speak but also by what they leave unspoken. If you are perceptive and have a high empathy quotient, you will understand the subtext behind what people say by tuning in to their choice of words. Notice how people tend to get disappointed or upset when someone tells them, "You are looking good today." In a sense, it implies that they don't look on most other days.

This is also one of the passive-aggressive statements often used for disarming people without sounding overtly caustic or mean. Another implication can also be that you look nice on other days but look particularly appealing on certain days.

If you want to build more significant empathy reserves, learn to listen to people carefully while also tuning in to read what is left unspoken. Several times, you'll notice people say something that isn't in tandem with their body language. This gives you more significant insights into people's feelings and emotions. Learn to stay more observant and pick up less than obvious signals used by people to communicate their innermost feelings and emotions. This will give you a clear advantage in boosting your empathy factor and understanding people's emotions.

Developing empathy doesn't imply being party to people's emotional drama. Of course, there is a flip side to it when certain people overdo it, and their woes and negative feelings completely take you over. Being empathetic and emotionally intelligent is about listening to people, offering suggestions or advice whenever required, extending understanding, and letting people know you know how they feel in a particular situation. Empathy is more about understanding things from a person's perspective and less about letting them impact your own emotions and feelings.

Extending empathy naturally comes when you begin with yourself. Start showing more compassion to yourself by understanding what you feel certain things the way you do. What makes you think, feel, or behave in a particular manner. You may not find instant answers. However, if you continue observing your feelings, you will slowly begin identifying several possibilities for why you experience a particular emotion.

Here are some tips for building greater empathy for being an effective communicator

1. Traveling and gaining exposure to multiple cultures, lifestyles, civilizations, and ethnicities is a beautiful way to start working on your empathy muscle. You'll not just develop cross-cultural skills but also be an ace when it comes to deciphering others' attitudes, ways of life, aspirations, fears, and beliefs. This will help you appreciate and varied perspectives. You will develop greater understanding, appreciation, and acceptance of people who are different from you. Plus, you will also gather more insights into how other people think and feel and articulate these thoughts, feelings, and emotions. Get exposed to as many viewpoints and ways of life as possible to appreciate and celebrate differences for boosting your empathy.

Another critical aspect of developing higher empathy is to examine your prejudices and biases. Daily, we deal with plenty of evident and veiled tendencies. Most of these biases run so deep that we aren't even aware of them. Preferences are the most giant stumbling blocks where empathy is concerned. It poses a challenge for listening to people with an open mind, understanding where they are coming from, and empathizing with their stand or situation.

Begin by making a detailed list of your biases. Try to gather as much evidence, details, and opinions that pose a challenge to your prejudices. Work with a more open mind. It helps to hold a broader worldview while communicating with people. People seldom like interacting with a person who is firmly fixated on his/her views as if theirs is the only way of looking at it. Keeping an open and flexible approach is essential from the perspective of being empathetic and an effective communicator.

Develop a natural and constructive curiosity in learning more about people and personalities. It helps to be a people analyzer, not because you want to play FBI with everyone you meet (although that doesn't hurt, either). However, this is more about learning from people without labeling or classifying them according to your own biases or preconceived notions. One of the biggest obstacles to effective communication is learning from people by keeping an open mind and lively curiosity. Look to learn from people in the most challenging situations if you want to become an effective communicator. You will find yourself changing your perception of different personalities and people by viewing them in a more positive and balanced manner. This will, in turn, boost your sense of appreciation for others, even in situations where you don't necessarily agree with them.

There is this game that I love to play when I am all by myself at the airport, doctors, café, and so on. I play this excellent little guessing game with myself to predict how someone will react or respond to a situation by putting myself in their shoes. In a way, this increases my understanding of the individual's feelings and emotions. Get into the habit of staying mindful and mentally present while people are talking. Instead of taking mental notes and constructing responses (more on listening skills later), keenly listen to people to increase your empathy and understand them more effectively.

Chapter 19: No Violent Communication

Stuff is bound to flare up in your relationships. There will be times when things become so thick people cannot see eye to eye, and this is when nonviolent communication (NVC) will come into play.

NVC prevents conflicts from taking place by establishing a foundation of respect and trust when people communicate. The beauty of NVC is that even at the point when you feel most angry and ready to flare up; or when your initial response will be overboard because you were angry, NVC causes you to act in a trusting and respectful manner, without a hint of passive aggression that typically causes resentment and distrust.

By definition, NVC is a communication framework designed to reduce conflict and tension among the people. It provides us with a lens that gives us an entirely different perspective of the world. It also changes how people express themselves to others, connect and communicate with others, and how they empathize with them. Essentially, NVC enables you to create a better, higher quality connection so that people may enjoy being in a relationship that has mutually beneficial outcomes.

Below are a few of the features of an NVC:

Peaceful Resolution of Conflicts

Conflicts are a normal part of interacting and relating with other people. Still, the important thing is to resolve them peacefully and productively, and this process requires some considerable time, support, and lots of practice. Peaceful conflict resolution engages both parties and has them working together to de-escalate, process, and resolve a conflict situation.

In this case, rather than confronting each other or burying the conflict as a whole, feuding persons are encouraged to demonstrate courage by opening up to each other regarding the conflict and how it affected them. They are also asked to show compassion to each other's side of the story, empathizing with the other party's experiences or interpretation of the events. Thirdly, the parties are asked to work together, in collaboration, to process the conflict and to come up with a resolution plan.

Here are the guidelines that help to chatter the way as you work towards resolving your cOnflict in a peaceful, healthy, and kind way, even in very tense circumstances:

Remain calm: remember that you control your emotions and not the other way. You must be able to manage your anger emotions before you can help another person manage his. Whichever method you use, from breathing deeply to others, you may have up your sleeve, the idea here is to keep your emotions under wraps long enough to allow negotiation.

There are no winners: sometimes, the conflict will revolve around a ridiculous issue of little or no consequence. For example, don't get caught up in dispute regarding a football match that happened or even one that is going to happen. Although fans can be very passionate, the players determine which team wins and which ones lose by playing in the field. As fans, you have to sit back and watch. Don't lose your peace over things you have no control over, especially those that do not require your participation. Also, do not fear to submit to another's opinions regarding issues like these because they do not influence your life in the first place.

Give the audience to the other party: If someone makes you part of an uncomfortable conversation, allow them to speak as much as they need to. Acting disinterested or interrupting them while they will not work in your favor only aggravates the situation. Remember that the person is not rational at the time, and he can pull you in that direction. Therefore, give him time to get everything off his system, and eventually, things will calm down.

Do not engage in verbal insults: when resolving a conflict, be watchful of your tone and the words you use. Avoid abusive or angry words; let your inner voice do the work. Audibly speaking profanity, screaming, and using hateful language only escalates the conflict.

Maintain a safe and comfortable distance: If you fear that the situation could quickly deteriorate and turn physical, keep a safe space from the other person. This will keep the person from attacking you or from interpreting your physical moves as offensive postures. Therefore, keep your distance and do not give room for the other person to feel threatened.

Overall, when you want to resolve a conflict peacefully, seek higher ground. Ask yourself, "Is it better to be right or happy?" From there, you will quickly figure out what you need to do.

Reconciliation after a Conflict

After a conflict, reconciliation allows parties to return to working together to build the society and achieve shared goals. Parties must begin to move past their divided opinions into a shared future. Reconciliation is meant to restore the relationship between people to allow for future engagements and collaborations. Unfortunately, reconciliation can be quite tricky, mainly because there are so many setbacks and failures involved, depending on the conflict's depth. However, the only real loss would be if the parties involved did not consider reconciliation.

There is no actual systematic process that parties can follow to resolve a conflict; each situation demands a unique approach. However, there are some lessons you could carry away to help you determine the rows in your life:

Reconciliation is both the process and the destination.

Reconciliation cannot be done in haste because it takes time to address the underlying issues such as anger, pain, frustration, etc.

Reconciliation processes should not be judged as either successes or failures because each process will have its micro wins and victories.

Reconciliation is done in several stages, and parties should expect relapses too.

Mutual interests can be beneficial in facilitating reconciliation between feuding parties.

With the understanding that reconciliation does not involve specific steps, parties should, however, ensure that both sides are heard. Parties must also be ready to abandon their old beliefs.

Secrets of Mediating Knowledge

There will be situations where the only thing feuding parties can agree on is that they need a mediator's help. The mediator ought to be a neutral party, whose role is not to judge and declare the winner and the loser. His goal is to help the parties come to an understanding.

Mediation takes place in two stages. The first stage is the joint session. Mediation begins by holding a meeting that lets the mediator in the prevailing situation. The parties present their facts, and each side indicates what its ideal resolution of the case would be. The mediator also needs to have all the information regarding what started the conflict and where it has gotten.

The second stage is the caucus stage, and in this one, the mediator is obliged to hold separate sessions with each party. The meeting's details should be highly confidential, but for the statements that the first party would want to be repeated to the second party. The mediator then collects each side's interests, including information about the concerns and needs that the dispute is affecting.

Once the second stage is done, the mediator begins moving from one party to another, collecting proposals and suggestions that the parties believe will equally satisfy their interests. Ultimately, a solution is reached. Sometimes, it will be a one-sided victory, while other times, it will end in a 'win-win' situation.

Making Bad Thoughts Disappear

When evil thoughts plague your mind, close your eyes as tightly as you can, do not shut them out. The idea or the feeling keeps popping up, over and over. The thoughts could be of a disturbing story you heard on the news, nagging self-doubt, or opinions of your relationship that went sour. All these thoughts make you miserable and cause you to feel imprisoned by your cruel mind.

Some people believe in the divine and will invoke their deities' power to drive the negative thoughts away, while the second group thinks nothing can be done about it. They believe that these thoughts have to come up and that blocking them out is only a waste of time. The good news is that you can totally block out unproductive thoughts, but only when armed with the right strategies.

You must remember that blocking out the negative thoughts is an effort in futility because the views rebound one way or another. Later on, when your guard is down, the idea comes back with the vengeance of a battalion, and suddenly, all you can think about are the negative thoughts. However, it is possible to block out the negative thoughts and not have any rebounds; you only need to remember two things.

The first is that blocking the thought is difficult, but just because it is difficult does not mean that you need to think about it. Your brain is not out to get you with the negativities. Stop thinking about the difficulty of letting the thoughts go because it is this thinking gives the idea more meaning and importance, making it even more challenging to get rid of.

The second step is to know how to handle negative thoughts when it shows up. The solution is to plan, in advance, what to do when the idea comes to mind. Some opt to ignore it, while others choose to replace the negative thought with some positive ones.

Using Positive Language

Language is quite a powerful tool, and how you express yourself affects how it is received, whether positively or negatively. Positive language is so useful it is used to convey even bad news. It also elicits cooperation and reception, unlike negative language that arouses confrontation and argument. In your daily communication, positive language helps project a positive, helpful image, while negative language projects a bad idea.

You must have come across a naysayer in the course of your life. A naysayer is a person who criticizes ideas, always having an opinion about why an image won't work. Sometimes, the naysayer won't even have a negative attitude; they will just speak using words or a tone that implies negativity. If you have been around someone like that, you know just how annoying and mentally fatiguing a person like that can be.

Since naysayers get creative by the day, here is how you identify negative language: it carries the message that you cannot do something, it subtly blames you, it does not mention or stress the positive consequences, and it includes words like can't, unable to, won't, and other words that let the listener or the reader know what cannot be done.

Positive language, on the other hand, will tell you what can be done. It will sound encouraging or helpful than bureaucratic, offer suggestions of possible alternatives, and stresses the positive actions or consequences that the reader or listener should expect. You certainly would want to lean towards positive language so that you can be a fountain of hope and positivity for others. Take up positive language and positive thinking, and replace all your negative statements with positive ones.

Chapter 20: Importance of Silence

Silence is significant in people's lives. It plays a vital role in us. Through silence, a person can think critically, get people to act, take away frustration from the mind, and slow down the reason.

Reasons why you should Try Silence

Bypassing Burnout

Being silent in a quiet place lets you break from productivity. This helps the body to rest, and in return, productivity is increased.

Heightened Sensitivity

Researchers have found out that increased silence by not talking increases alertness in other areas.

Avoiding Future Problems

According to Alan Watts, our anxiety and frustrations are anchored on disconnection- existing in the future.

Silence brings us to the current time other than the future.

Memory improvement

Silence, combined with walking in nature, improves the memory of the brain.

Increased Self-Awareness

Solitude allows us to reflect on our lives, and this way, we increase our self-awareness. This will, in turn, lead to control.

Brain Growth

Research has shown that time spent in silence increases people's ability to digest information. Setting aside at least ten minutes to be in silence helps in the growth of the brain.

Emotional Cleansing

Sitting in silence has proved to help lower emotional turbulence that builds up in the mind. You can reflect and think about what brought about the bad emotions.

Activities that promote Silence

-Taking a walk in a quiet place.

-Painting or drawing.

-Arts and crafts

-Coloring

-Arts and crafts.

Listening is an art

Learning to listen is a crucial element in a successful conversation. As mentioned above, nobody likes it if all you do is talk without asking how someone else is, how they are, what is going on in their life, and just generally asking about the other person. A successful conversation means both parties are active participants, both parties talk and listen, and the message communicated has been understood in the same context. When speaking, we become both the talker and the listener, just at two different times. Here is how you can master both:

When you are making the talking, take note of the following;

Think straight

Muddled thinking is the leading cause of confusing messages. Most of the time, when we have an idea, we do not think properly about it. Either that, or we just have plenty to say but do not know how to convey it properly. When this happens, we come across as ill-prepared when talking, our ideas and thoughts are not conveyed properly, and we end up confusing everyone. To prevent this, the first thing is to think before saying a thing critically. In this way, you would articulate your ideas better and organize what you think about, thus conveying a clear and concise message.

Mean what you say

Quit the confusing jargon and big words. Tell someone what you exactly mean when you communicate. You'd be surprised how a simple sentence can convey your message across more beautifully than hard to understand, long sentences.

Go straight to the point.

When you do not get to the point, you're not only wasting the other person's time but yours as well. If you want to communicate effectively:

Get straight to the point.

Make your objectives clear, and what is the purpose of the conversation. If you want something, ask for it.

If you need help, ask. If you want something explained, seek out help.

Be concise

By not getting to the point, adding so many words in your sentence, or stretching the conversation, all you are doing is creating confusion. The more terms used, the greater the confusion. Speak using short and familiar names.

Be authentic

To ensure clarity of your message and goals, be authentic in your presentation of your message. Use your personality, and just be you when you speak. Of course, you need to take into context the situation you are in. For example, if you are doing a client presentation, be polite and confident but not stuffy and stuck up. Allow the real you shine because, in this way, you will be more resounding and comfortable when you convey your thoughts and ideas.

Stopping to Look and Listen

Looking and listening are crucial admonitions in conversations. We all know how images can paint a thousand words. So when speaking, you can also help the receiver of your message visualize your content by giving examples or even using facial expressions and gestures. Listen to social cues around you when speaking help you convey a message and helps the listener understand what you are saying.

When you are doing the listening, take note of the following;

Listen with care and thought-

Like writing and speaking, listening also requires genuine attention and interest. You will not be learning much if you do not actively listen and, the rate of remembering anything will not be very high either. According to research, we remember 25 percent of the things that we hear. Therefore, if you want to raise your retention rate and your understanding of something, you need to increase listening effectiveness.

Use your eyes- The eyes are the windows to our soul, and if you only use your ears to listen, you miss out on understanding the message. To become a good and active listener, you also need to activate your eyes to look at what the speaker says. This not only enhances the listening, but it also shows or tells the speaker that you are genuinely interested in what is being said. Our face is a communication medium, and we use it to learn to interpret messages that are both verbal and non-verbal. The look can say many things, so we must convey our attention through the non-verbal cues on our face and eyes.

Observing nonverbal signals

Nonverbal cues are incredibly crucial when trying to read someone because, in many ways, you can detect if someone is lying or if they are enjoying a date, or how they are as a person when they come in for a job interview. It is about reading between the lines to accurately interpret body language to know if the person's words convey how they genuinely feel.

Being Funny

You may think that being funny is a gift, but it's not. Being funny is simply the ability to be living in the present moment, trust that your timing will be right on, and have the creative ability to look at things and mention them in unexpected ways and say something about it.

That's all it is. You don't have to memorize a hundred jokes.

Being funny has a lot to do with timing. Once you get the hang of it, it gets easier and easier, and then before you know it, it's almost as if your friends will be waiting for your next funny remark – they will get to expect it and almost eagerly look at you to see what you're going to say next. When you listen to your gut instinct, have fun, and let go of worry, your timing will be perfect, and you will never be without the right words.

Being funny is really about trusting yourself and your intuition to feed you funny things to say at the perfect moment. When you are having fun and in a state of peace and balance already, and when you live in the moment, being present, being funny comes very easy and natural.

Chapter 21: Cognitive Behavioral Approach

Cognitive Behavioral Therapy (CBT)

Cognitive Behavioral Therapy works by emphasizing the relationship between our thoughts, feelings, and behaviors. When you begin to change any of these components, you start to initiate change in the others. CBT aims to help lower the amount of worry you do and increase your life's overall quality. Here are the 8 fundamental principles of how Cognitive Behavioral Therapy works:

CBT will help provide a new perspective of understanding your problems.

Often, when an individual has been living with a problem for a long time in their life, they may have developed unique ways of understanding it and dealing with it. Usually, this just maintains the problem or makes it worse. CBT is useful in helping you look at your situation from a new perspective, and this will help you learn other ways of understanding your situation and learning a new way of dealing with it.

CBT will help you generate new skills to work out your problem.

You probably know that understanding a problem is one matter, and dealing with it is entirely another can of worms. To help start changing your situation, you will need to develop new skills to change your thoughts, behaviors, and emotions that affect your anxiety and mental health. For instance, CBT will help you achieve new ideas about your problem and begin to use and test them in your daily life. Therefore, you will be more capable of making up your mind regarding the root issue causing these negative symptoms.

CBT relies on teamwork and collaboration between the client and therapist (or program).

CBT will require you to be actively involved in the entire process, and your thoughts and ideas are precious right from the beginning of the therapy. You are the expert when it comes to your thoughts and problems. The therapist is the expert when it comes to acknowledging the emotional issues. By working as a team, you will identify your questions and have your therapist better address them. Historically, the more the therapy advances, the more the client finds techniques to deal with the symptoms.

The goal of CBT is to help the client become their therapist.

Therapy is expensive; we all know that. One of CBT's goals is not to have you become overly dependent on your therapist because it is not feasible to have therapy forever. When treatment comes to an end, and you do not become your therapist, you will be at high risk for a relapse.

However, if you can become your therapist, you will be in a good spot to face the hurdles that life throws at you. It is also proven that having confidence in your ability to face hardship is one of the best predictors of maintaining the valuable information you got from therapy. By playing an active role during your sessions, you will gain the confidence needed to face your problems when the sessions are over.

CBT is brief and time-limited.

As a rule of thumb, CBT therapy sessions typically last for 10 to 20 sessions. Statistically, when therapy goes on for many months, there is a higher risk of the client becoming dependent on the therapist. Once you have gained a new perspective and understanding of your problem and are equipped with the right skills, you can use them to solve future problems. It is crucial in CBT for you to try out your new skills in the real world. By actually dealing with your own problem hands-on without the security of recurring therapy sessions, you will be able to build confidence in your ability to become your therapist.

CBT is direction based and structured.

CBT typically relies on a fundamental strategy called 'guided recovery.' By setting up some experiments with your therapist, you will be able to experiment with new ideas to see if they reflect your reality accurately. In other words, your therapist is your guide while you are making discoveries in CBT. The therapist will not tell you whether you are right or wrong, but instead, they will help develop ideas and experiments to test these ideas.

CBT is based on the present, "here and now."

Although we know that our childhood and developmental history play a significant role in who we are today, one of CBT's principles distinguishes between what caused the problem and what maintains the problem presently. In many cases, the reasons that support a problem are different from those originally caused it.

For example, if you fall off while riding a horse, you may become afraid of horses. Your fear will continue to be maintained if you begin avoiding all horses and refusing to ride one again. In this example, the fear was called by the fall, but you are continuing to maintain it by avoiding your fear. Unfortunately, you cannot change the fact that you had fallen off the horse, but you can change your behaviors when it comes to avoidance. CBT primarily focuses on the factors that are maintaining the problem because these factors are susceptible to change.

Worksheet exercises are significant elements of CBT therapy.

Unfortunately, reading about CBT or going to one therapy session a week is not enough to change our ingrained patterns of thinking and behaving. During CBT, the client is always encouraged to apply their new skills into their daily lives. Although most people find CBT therapy sessions very intriguing, it does not lead to change in reality if you do not exercise the skills you have learned.

These eight principles will be your guiding light throughout your Cognitive Behavioral Therapy. By learning, understanding, and applying these eight principles, you will be in an excellent position to invest your time and energy into becoming your therapist and achieving your personal goals.

Based on research, individuals who are highly motivated to try exercises outside of sessions tend to find more value in therapy than those who don't. Keep in mind that other external factors still affect your success, but your motivation is one of the most significant factors. By following CBT using the principles above, you should be able to remain highly motivated throughout CBT.

Challenging Your Unhelpful Thinking Styles

Once you can identify your unhelpful thinking styles, you can begin trying to reshape those thoughts into something more realistic and factual. Here, we will be learning how to challenge these thoughts to build a healthier thinking style.

Keep in mind that it takes a lot of effort and dedication to change our thoughts, so don't get frustrated if you fail right away. You probably have had these thoughts for a while, so don't expect it to change overnight.

Probability Overestimation

If you find that you have thoughts about a possible negative outcome, but you are noticing that you often overestimate the probability, try asking yourself the questions below to re-evaluate your beliefs.

Based on my experience, what is the probability that this thought will come true realistically?

What are the other possible results from this situation? Is the outcome that I am thinking of now the only possible one? Does my feared work have the highest probability out of the other outcomes?

Have I ever experienced this type of situation before? If so, what happened? What have I learned from these past experiences that would be helpful to me now?

If a friend or loved one is having these thoughts, what would I say to them?

Catastrophizing

If the prediction that I am afraid of really did come true, how bad would it be?

If I am feeling embarrassed, how long will this last? How long will other people remember/talk about it? What are all the different things they could be saying? Is it 100% that they will only think bad things?

I am feeling uncomfortable right now, but is this a horrible or unbearable outcome?

What are the other alternatives for how this situation could turn out?

If a friend or loved one was having these thoughts, what would I say to them?

Mind Reading

Is it possible that I know what other people's thoughts are? What are the other things they could be thinking about?

Do I have any evidence to support my assumptions?

In the scenario that my assumption is true, what is so bad about it?

Personalization

What other elements might be playing a role in the situation? Could it be the other person's stress, deadlines, or mood?

Does somebody always have to be at blame?

A conversation is never just one person's responsibility.

Were any of these circumstances out of my control?

Should Statements

Would I be holding the same standards to a loved one or a friend?

Are there any exceptions?

Will someone else does this differently?

All or Nothing Thinking

Is there a middle ground or a grey area that I am not considering?

Would I judge a friend or loved one in the same way?

Was the entire situation 100% negative? Was there any part of the situation that I handled well?

Is having/showing some anxiety such a horrible thing?

Selective Attention/Memory

What are the positive elements of the situation? Am I ignoring those?

Would a different person see this situation differently?

What strengths do I have? Am I ignoring those?

Negative Core Beliefs

Do I have any evidence that supports my negative beliefs?

Is this thought true in every situation?

Would a loved one or friend agree with my self-belief?

Once you catch yourself using these unhelpful thinking patterns, ask yourself the above questions to begin changing your thoughts. Remember, CBT's core basis is that your thoughts affect your emotions, influencing your behavior. By catching and changing your thoughts before it spirals, you will be in control of your emotions and behavior as well.

Chapter 22: Conversational Mistakes

We've just gone over some clear, conversational no-nos in the workplace. In more social settings, these don't apply so strictly. Nevertheless, talk about sex, religion, and politics are generally fraught topics. In any situation, one needs to be sensitive to others' feelings about these topics. Let's go over some finer details about touchy subjects. We'll then look at some common speech patterns that lessen your impact as an engaging conversationalist.

Part of me resists using the term' political correctness' as it seems such a loaded term. It conjures up a visceral and politically volatile reaction, regardless of what your politics are. We can see how the surfacing of certain terms puts people into a defensive position, bracing for a battle played out on lines that far predate whatever the current moment is. Certain terms and phrases are just like that. They cause people to draw sabers, and then any chance of conversation fades away as the blades get sharpened and readied to thrust and parry.

This isn't a value judgment but a simple observation. We all have certain fiercely held beliefs and are prepared to battle to defend them. And there's always a time and place to have those battles. But even in warfare, there are accepted conventions that warring parties observe. Well, they're observed more or less.

How we use words, and the words we choose, are rife with deep histories and embody real ideas that reflect and actively shape the world we live in. Language is very much one of the battlefields where politics are conducted. But unless we want to spend all our time talking pointlessly with others in various states of agitation and conflict, it's necessary, at the very least, to be aware of this function of language as a shaper as well as a describer of the world we all share.

Treating others with the respect and dignity we wish to be treated with requires it. Yet honesty is also the foundation of any meaningful and useful conversation. So, if someone uses an offensive racial epithet in my presence, should I ignore it for the sake of comity?

There's rarely a clear, certain answer in such a situation. The conversation is an art as much as a science. However, we can follow a few basic rules to help us find that wisdom that determines when a battle approaches are worth fighting and what terms will be fought.

First, even when one has to be seriously offended, it's rarely useful to respond with both barrels blazing. It's tempting to escalate and retaliate with devastating, ad hominem attacks, but it rarely accomplishes anything. Say you're a white male in a casual conversation with another white male when suddenly he drops an n-bomb, out of nowhere, as if testing you to see if you hold his racist views. This has happened to me a few times. Well, what are your options? Do you call him a racist moron? Do you simply walk away? Do you try to engage him, force him to defend his racist views? Or do you explain how you find his language deeply offensive? Or do you pretend as if he never said the thing at all and continue talking?

There's no easy answer. I could see myself following any four possible responses, depending upon the specific circumstances, not least how I was generally feeling that moment. And really, the correct one is dependent upon many factors too numerous to list here, certainly too numerous to form any kind of one size fits all rule. The conversation is just like that. The rules of warfare are often unclear when two sides are trying to kill each other.

Let's de-escalate the scenario now. Let's imagine the guy I'm talking with said something much less offensive than an appalling racist epithet, maybe something that merely annoyed me. For instance, we're in Los Angeles at a convention, and I was born in the Midwest. He commented about 'flyover country,' the hicks out there or something. People will often display their ignorance in the course of conversation.

But in this instance, it's not quite as offensive or emotionally charged. The stakes aren't quite so high, though I do feel a desire to educate him or make a cutting remark, maybe. What's the correct line to take?

Let's de-escalate even further. Let's say the guy just remarked when the Yankees won the World Series in 1990. I'm a baseball fan, and I know the Yankees didn't even come close to winning the World Series in 1990. But I just found out he's a baseball fan too. I'm in the mood to talk about baseball. Maybe we'll overlook his ignorance of the 1990 season, the playoffs are going, and I'm rooting for my team, and I'm curious to know who he's rooting for. I think I'll ignore his statement.

There is an infinite number of scenarios between these three examples. There are various gradations of expertise, strong belief, and ignorance in all three. And the stakes are different in all three as well. The point at which words or a single word is charged with political significance is a point on a moving spectrum. It's one of the reasons why conversation is such a unique and exciting human occupation. As we speak with others, we're not only opening ourselves up to new knowledge; we're influencing those we're speaking with. It's an essential human activity since it plays out in the realm of language. How we use language is important. It not only communicates but helps us shape the world we live in.

Perhaps the biggest mistake we can make is not engaging at all. Simply ignoring the racist comment isn't an option for me personally. The second biggest mistake I could make would be to recognize that my words have historical and political meanings in and of themselves. That part of what we do when engaging in conversation is battle over what those meanings are.

Words That Don't Mean Anything

Let's now think about a serious conversational crime we're all guilty of to some degree or other. That's using words that mean absolutely nothing. Um, you know, like, what I'm trying to say, is maybe…words, that you know, I mean, like, words that don't do a damn thing in expressing your thought other than show you don't know what you're talking about and that maybe you need to buy a book on how to hold up your end of a conversation. Or whatever.

Again, we're all guilty of this at times. It's fair to say the number one offender is 'you know.' No, I don't know. That's why I'm waiting for you to get to the point. You know, nobody enjoys talking with someone who doesn't know, you know—or talking with someone who assumes that you know what he doesn't know because he can't seem to come out with it, you know. If I already know, why are you trying to tell me? Wouldn't it be better to say 'you don't know,' you know if you're trying to tell me something you haven't yet said?

The current permutations of 'you know' are endless. My second favorite is the inimitable 'like,' which we use as an odd poetic twitch. I'm going to meet with her, like, next Friday night. That's different than meeting with her next Friday night. That 'like' is, like, telling me how very I have no idea what it's telling me other than the guy who's speaking to me needs to work on his speech patterns.

There's also 'whatever,' which apparently can indicate either dismissal or be open to anything, two almost exactly opposite ideas. I mean, whatever.

And there's also the near limitless utility of 'basically.' I was, like, basically fired. My girlfriend is pregnant. That car that hit me and took off was red. And now my leg is broken. It is a charming word, which means its exact opposite, which is to say it means nothing other than it is a word you should cease using.

The list could go on, but I think you get the point.

Strive to say exactly what you mean, and people will know you mean exactly what you say.

So how do you break the habit of these poor speech habits? Try using one of our three 'basic' skills, listening, but to yourself, as you speak. You'll probably see you're also using a whole repertoire of us and has and us as well. Try monitoring yourself next time you're in any low-stress social situation. You'll get started improving by becoming aware of how often your mind resorts to these filler words. Examine the evidence for yourself.

Next, strive to think ahead just a moment before you comment. This is just a flash of a moment. Look at the entire sentence before it comes spilling out of your mouth. What often trips us up is that we tend to be forming the following sentence before we've finished speaking the present one. Perhaps you'll have a nanosecond of a gap between sentences, but nobody will even notice. Also, look closely at the speech patterns of an accomplished television interviewer. Imagine what they'd sound like if their speech were filled with filler words.

If you have a close partner, you might even have the 'buzz' you for a few days. Tell them they should say 'buzzzzz" every time they hear you using a dreaded filler word. They'll probably enjoy that exercise immensely.

Chapter 23: How to Use Feedback

Asking For Feedback

One of the most worn-out pieces of advice you'll come across when trying to improve your communication skills is this phrase: "Ask for feedback." Ironically, hardly do people ever implement it correctly! And the reason is not far-fetched: most people ask for feedback most ineffectively.

Feedback is essential for correction, assessment, and improvement. But unless you are a subordinate or under someone's authority (such as a child/parent or student/teacher relationship), it is usually difficult to get honest feedback. A person in a lower position gets feedback whether or not they ask for it. But the reverse is often the case for people in higher positions. For example, it is rare to find a student telling their teacher what they truly think about the teacher's methods. It is not every day that you see a subordinate boldly walk up to their boss to share their candid opinion about their unpopular leadership style.

Here's a scenario you might be familiar with. A new boss is transferred to your department. He or she ends their inaugural speech with the cliché, "feel free to let me know if I need to make corrections." Unfortunately, no one – at least, those below the boss' rank – will ever dare to speak up even when they are uncomfortable with some of the new changes.

This is not common for people of lesser rank or authority to "feel free" in giving feedback to their superior, especially if it is critical feedback. So stop asking for it! That approach doesn't work.

Asking for feedback in work situations can be tricky, but you can pull it off with the right skills. Perhaps the real-life story of Sheryl Sandberg of Facebook might help you understand this point better. Sandberg established a rule of interviewing each member of her team when she first started working at Google. To her, it was important to know every person she worked with. At first, it was an easy thing to do because she had just a handful of people on her team. But with time, her team grew exponentially, and it was taking forever to interview everyone. She held a meeting with her direct reports and informed them that she was considering stopping the interviews. She had expected them to oppose her suggestion because the interview was a crucial part of the process.

Here's the truth: honest feedback doesn't usually come in a pleasant format. For this reason, most people do not feel comfortable giving feedback to someone higher in rank or position. If you are a leader of some sort (whether at work or home), you need to understand that no one under you would want to be seen as challenging your authority. So, you have to encourage your subordinates, direct reports, or those under you to air their views. But avoid using the traditional "feel free to let me know" style.

Giving Feedback

Have you ever heard of the "shit sandwich?" It is a method of communicating critical feedback without hurting the receiver's feelings. Typically, the shit sandwich follows this pattern. It begins with some form of praise or commendation, which is then followed by negative feedback. It ends with a commendation. In other words, you are sandwiching critical feedback between praises. For example, "I can see how determined you are about perfecting your drumming skills. That's a great thing. But you need to devote more time to your homework. Your grades are taking a nosedive, and that's not a good thing. I know you can do better because you are naturally good at anything you set your mind to."

On the surface, this seems like a great technique for communicating critical feedback, right? Well, let me save you the headache of trying to learn how to deliver the shit sandwich because it can be easily overused and quickly become ineffective. Here's the disadvantage of the shit sandwich. Anytime you start to give praise, the receiver knows what will come next. Your praises become empty noise with little to no positive impact because it is certain that something unpleasant will follow the praise. Those in your circle – your family, friends, and colleagues – will sooner or later start to loathe your praises. Pretty soon, someone bold will cut you off when you start to praise them and say something like, "Just cut to the chase!"

Keep in mind that honest feedback doesn't necessarily mean negative or critical feedback. Do not downplay people's strengths and overemphasize their weaknesses. A good communicator seeks to bring out the best in those he or she relates to. It doesn't matter whether who occupies a higher status – you or your parent, boss, direct report, friend, and so on – get in the habit of giving honest, positive feedback. Don't let people get used to thinking that you are about to lash them each time you have a one-on-one with them.

Chapter 24: Conversations and Effective Communication

Conversations and Communication

Conversations are exchanges of verbal and nonverbal messages between two or more people and constitute the main way of communicating and relating to others, sharing thoughts, opinions, and feelings.

Although almost all of us can hold conversations, our ability to develop in them can differ quite a bit. There are people with whom we feel like talking. It is easy to communicate and others with whom the opposite happens. Being a good conversationalist is very important, both to initiate relationships of various kinds and maintain them and make them productive and satisfying.

The ability to talk and communicate with others is an antidote against social isolation. This is important since loneliness and lack of communication often produce negative emotions and predispose them to emotional disturbances such as anxiety or depression. Instead, the ability to communicate and feel supported by other people improves our mood and our ability to manage stress or overcome any adversity. Interpersonal communication also helps us get to know ourselves better and improve our self-esteem and emotional intelligence.

Non-Assertive Attitudes When Initiating, Maintaining, or Closing Conversations

Some people tend to be inhibited: avoiding as much as possible the beginning or maintenance of conversations, speaking little, avoiding expressing their opinions or feelings, and letting others take the initiative always. This attitude leads them to lose many opportunities to communicate, establish relationships, get what they want, and feel bad about themselves.

On the contrary, other people maintain "aggressive" attitudes when communicating since they do not respect the rules, talk too much, interrupt others, always want to be the center of attention, and try to impose their interests and opinions. This usually results in the rejection of others. Inhibited or aggressive attitudes toward maintaining conversations are usually based on irrational ideas.

Start Conversations

As Galassi points out, we have the right to communicate and talk with other people when we are interested or want to. Most people like to talk to others and, therefore, tend to respond favorably when we try to communicate with them. But when others do not want it, the right thing is that we recognize their right to act like this and respect it, without trying to force them to talk or communicate with us.

In the first phase, the most important thing is the nonverbal language, both yours and that of the other person. Before starting a conversation, it is interesting to observe the other's nonverbal language to deduce if he is more or less willing to talk. It is also important to take care of your body language: trying to show interest and pleasure, showing you friendly and relaxed, looking, smiling, and taking care of the verbal and nonverbal tuning with your interlocutor.

We have the right to communicate with others when we are interested or want to do so. The most appropriate way to start a conversation will depend on the situation; your goals and purposes (e.g., knowing the other person); the objectives and interests of your interlocutor, and the social rules implicit in each situation.

Usually, a greeting or introduction is made, and then a comment or question is asked about something pleasant, positive, or that you think may interest the other. Some concrete forms and examples would be:

Greet the other person by saying: "Hello! How are you? How are you?," etc., or introduce yourself, saying: "Hello! My name is ..., and I am ... "(giving you some information about yourself that may interest you).

Talk about topics to break the ice: "What a bad weather today."

Make a comment or a question about the situation in which the conversation occurs, such as: "What a beautiful landscape you can see from here!" Ask if you can join the activity carried out by the other or if the other wants to join yours: "Do you want to sit with us?"

Make sincere compliments about the other or about the situation: "Your talk has been very interesting."

Offer something: "Do you fancy a drink?"

Ask for information, help, advice, or opinion: "Can you tell me the time?"

Be interested in the other one by asking a kind question: "I found your comment very interesting, why do you think ...?"; "It seems that you are looking for someone, can I help you?" etc.

How to Get Into an Already Started Conversation

When we want to participate in a conversation that other people are having, it is recommended to follow the following guidelines:

Think about whether it is appropriate for you to enter the conversation, taking into account: your objectives (e.g., if you find it necessary, desirable, etc.), the goals or desires of others, their nonverbal language, etc.

Observe before intervening to try to tune in to the people who are communicating.

As for the nonverbal language, it is usually useful:

Look at the speaker.

Make a hand gesture - for example, raise a hand as if asking permission to speak.

Position yourself so that you are visible to the group.

204

Position your body, arms, and feet facing the speaker, or touch his arm slightly.

Do not get into the conversation by interrupting the speaker. Do not try to change the subject or express your disagreement with others too soon or too sharply.

Hold Conversations

One of the main objectives is usually to make the talk pleasant and interesting when talking with someone. For this, it is very important to be aware of non-verbal language, both of our own and that of our interlocutor (to capture how he feels and how he reacts to what we say).

Once the conversation has started, there are several ways to keep it or expand it:

Comment and then ask the other person about their point of view on that topic. For example: "I found the book quite good; what do you think?"

Listen carefully to the other's responses or comments, capturing any detail that can be used to continue the conversation. It will surely offer you spontaneous information that helps you find common interest topics if you feel like talking to you.

Answer the interlocutor's questions by adding some additional information. So, if he asks you, "What part of the book did you like?"

Then, instead of simply answering laconically: "The first part," you can give a broader explanation, such as: "The first part; because it explains it in a very interesting and easy to understand way…," etc.

Also, give some personal information about what you like, dislike, etc. .; but taking care that it is not so personal that it seems out of place.

Do not talk excessively and respect the pauses in conversations.

Kelly considers that the main components of the ability to hold conversations are: adequate eye contact, emotional expression (being calm, warm, cordial, energetic, etc.), the duration of the interventions (that is not too short or long), the use of pertinent questions, information about oneself and the use of reinforcing comments (e.g., sincere praise).

Ending Conversations

Ending conversations assertively usually consists of knowing how to close them whenever we want and doing so in a pleasant and friendly way. We can consider two problematic attitudes: 1) that of those who tend to extend the conversation more than their interlocutor wants and, 2) that of those who are unable to cut the other, even if they are willing to do so. People in the first group, who extend their conversation too much, do not usually realize that the other is upset.

To prevent this from happening, it is convenient to be very aware of the interlocutor's non-verbal language (signs of discomfort, looks at the clock, grimaces, etc.) and any comment that indicates his desire to end the conversation. In case of doubt, we can ask: "Are you in a hurry?" "Would you rather we speak at another time?" etc.

As for people who have difficulty cutting the conversation (when their interlocutor insists on continuing to talk beyond what they won't), their attitude may be due to excessive fear of disturbing the other, shyness, or not knowing how to end assertive conversations.

Being able to end (properly) a conversation when we want it is an important skill. Otherwise, we lose the freedom to do what we want. We get in a bad mood, usually transmitted through our nonverbal language, making it difficult for effective communication.

Assertive Ways to End Conversations

Once we have a clear goal - to end the conversation without the interlocutor feeling annoyed - we can use some assertive way to do it, as in the following examples:

Communicate kindly that you want to finish: "Excuse me, but I have to go."

Summarize what we have talked about and express our desire to end the conversation: "Well, we have agreed that ... Do you think we will call each other as soon as we have news?"

Reinforce the other person, expressing some positive feelings towards her, before expressing our desire to end the conversation: "Whenever

I am with you, I have a great time, but I have pending work." Use nonverbal language: look at the clock, stand up, etc.

If the other asks if you are in a hurry, say clearly yes and sometimes list the things you have to do.

Defer the continuation of the conversation to another time, telling you, for example: "I'm sorry, but I have to go. Are we still talking tomorrow?"

What to Do If You're Interlocutor Refuses to End the Conversation?

Suppose your interlocutor tends to continue speaking after communicating your desire to end the conversation. In that case, you can gradually withdraw the eye contact and the signals that you are listening to him (e.g., stopping nod to your words). And, when you pause your speech, take the opportunity to repeat that you have to leave, that you will continue talking, etc.

If it takes too long to pause, you can say looking into his eyes and gently touching his arm: "I'm sorry, but I have to go" or "Sorry to interrupt you, but I have to finish this job," etc. In these cases, the non-verbal language is very important, which must be firm and kind. With some people, it is convenient that we stay to talk in their field (e.g., at home or in your office) or a neutral place, such as a cafeteria, because it will be easier for us to finish and leave than if the conversation takes place in our house or our office.

Chapter 25: Silly Mistakes to avoid

Often while communicating, especially in times of conflict, people will use communication means that can be considered "violent." While this does not mean physical violence, we can be violent in the way that we communicate. What this means is communicating in a way that results in harm to someone else or ourselves. Violent communication is a means of communication that includes any number of the following.

- Judging
- Shaming
- Criticizing
- Ridiculing
- Demanding
- Coercing
- Labeling
- Threatening
- Blaming
- Accusing

When any or all of the following are present in our communications, we are using violent communication. Communicating in this way has negative impacts on the people with whom we are communicating. As this is violent communication, it causes internal harm. If we are communicating interpersonally in this way, we may cause harm to ourselves. If we communicate in this way with others, we can cause internal harm to others. In time, this type of communication can lead to anger and resentment. If we speak to ourselves in this way, it can eventually lead to depression.

Often, we don't even know we are using violent communication. It may be quite a normal way of interacting for us. Many societies model violent communication, and thus, the people who grow up in them don't realize that there is any other way to communicate. This causes many interactions to be full of anger and hate and involve raised voices and harsh words. Sometimes, this leads to physical violence.

Violent communication aims to lower a person's feelings of self-worth, ignore their needs, and void compassion. It can happen on both the part of the speaker and the listener. Below are some examples of different forms of violent communication for your reference.

Moral Judgement or Evaluation

"Jennifer is lazy."

In this example, the speaker is using judgment. They are also labeling Jennifer and being critical of her. They are evaluating her and doing so in a judgmental way. In this type of violent communication, the speaker often sees the other person as being wrong.

Denying Responsibility

"It's not my fault; the policy states that I have to fire you."

In this example of violent communication, the speaker refuses to take responsibility for their actions and blame them on policies, regulations, and rules. In this example, the person may also blame their thoughts or feelings on other people or rules, social rules, or anything other than their decision-making.

Demanding

"You need to do my homework for me."

In this type of example, the speaker is implying (or sometimes explicitly stating) that there is the threat of punishment of having to take the blame or of losing a reward if they do not comply with the demand. This type can also be seen in the reverse, where there is a reward if the person complies with the demand. This is a manipulative form of communication, which is also a type of demand.

Lack of Compassion

"Were you sick yesterday, or did you just not feel like showing up?"

In this type of example, lacking compassion, there are numerous ways to show up in an interaction. At its core, this type of violent communication involves the speaker intentionally sounding like they are trying to fix a situation but doing so in a way that involves correcting the listener, shutting them down, trying to educate them, one-upping them, or interrogating them. In this way, the speaker does not show compassion but is trying to be the voice of reason where it was not solicited.

While the person communicating powerfully may not realize it, it can result in the listener following along with whatever the request is out of feelings of obligation, fear of punishment, shame, fear, or guilt. Thus, this type of communication can be quite manipulative and controlling, as it forces others' actions.

You may get what you want out of creating this type of situation. Still, the ways that it can impact your relationships and your mental health negatively are worth mentioning. Firstly, if you speak to others in this way, the chances you speak to yourself in this way are quite high. By not being compassionate or empathetic to others, you are likely unaware of how to be compassionate or empathetic to yourself. This means that your mental health and your emotional well-being will suffer. By learning how to use compassion and empathy toward others, you will learn how to use it in your intrapersonal interactions. Secondly, speaking violently toward others, it can cause your relationships to suffer. If you speak to your family members, such as your children, in this way, to get them to do what you want, they will more than likely develop feelings of resentment toward you. This becomes a discussion of whether it is worth it to you to have others' actions controlled by your words or if you would rather have steady and genuine relationships that don't involve fear, shame, and guilt.

Throughout all relationships, especially long-term ones, there is a high likelihood that you have had a huge argument with your partner that may have shattered your trust for them. This is normal and happens to the best of us. However, if you love this person and want to continue working on a relationship with them, you must learn to restore trust as mistrust will only lead to more problems. When a person's trust is broken, it often feels like they can no longer communicate with the other person as they now don't know whether they can be trusted with new information. This is normal. The trick to overcoming this is to force yourself to communicate, even if your thoughts surround the fact that you don't trust them.

The secret to this is all about HOW you communicate this with your partner. Saying phrases such as "I don't trust you anymore!" or "I can never trust you again!" is a form of violent communication and will only cause more distrust in your partner. Instead, communicate your mistrust to your partner in a way that they can emphasize with. For instance, you can say, "That incident has caused me to lose trust in you. It may take us some time to get back to where we were," or "I want to be able to trust you again, but we need some time to work on it." These are all ways to let your partner know that you have lost some trust in them, but you have not given up entirely on them.

It is also important to ask for what you need. If you need your partner to perform certain actions to help you gain the trust back, ask them, and let them know. Don't keep it to yourself. People can't read minds, so sitting there silently hoping that your partner will make it up to you somehow will only cause more resentment within yourself. Instead, communicate to them that there may be things they need to do for you for the trust to heal. It's all about open communication and the way you deliver your messages. Always use nonviolent communication in situations like this.

Chapter 26: How to Remember a Person's Name

The ability to quickly and permanently remember peoples' names is an extremely underrated skill and a must-have feature of anyone who wants to communicate effectively and smoothly! Remembering names will allow you to make an awesome first impression and save you lots of trouble after forgetting someone's name after five minutes of conversation.

Some time ago, remembering names was a great challenge for me. Usually, when two or three people told me their names, I forgot them after about a few minutes. I wanted to remember them, but they would just vanish rapidly. It very often held me back from making a good first impression and from succeeding at job interviews, during the first days at a new school, university, in a new company, during business meetings, or even during nights out with friends when I wanted to meet new people. From what I noticed, this is quite a popular problem. My dear friend almost lost the chance to have a date with the love of his life because he forgot her name and, after one hour of talking, called her Jennifer instead of Jessica. It ended up in a painful but funny (for us, not him) face slap since she is a rather fiery and impulsive kind of girl. Luckily, I eventually convinced her that he's a very good man, just a little bit forgetful. I'm going to show you a few tricks, thanks to which you will impress everyone with your great memory for names and improve your social skills.

Remembering a name and then using it early in the first conversations is one of the best ways to make a great first impression. Using the name of the person you just met will make them feel important to you. By doing so, you can easily open the door to creating a special relationship with that person.

"For most people, their name is the sweetest and most important sound in any language." - Dale Carnegie.

Here's how to go about it:

Commit Yourself

Decide today that you will remember names every time you meet someone new. Usually, when we talk to someone for the first time, we do not pay attention to their name. It usually disappears from our heads literally in a matter of seconds. That's why the commitment to start remembering the names of people you meet is so important.

If you think, "I have such a bad memory for names," then you are wrong and looking for excuses. There is no such thing as a bad memory for names. If you do not remember them, it means that you do nothing to remember them. Decide that from now on, you will start doing something in this direction. Recall that undertaking whenever you expect to meet someone new.

Focus

When you are greeting someone for the first time, always be focused on this activity. You need to be present at the moment. Dispersion and lack of focused attention will simply hold you back from remembering names. Carefully listen to what people say, how they introduce themselves. Moreover, take notice of how each person looks. See what characteristics their faces have. You will need these details to create associations, which I will describe in the fourth point.

Repeat

Repetition of the name is a quick way to save it in your memory. You can repeat names in many different ways. For example, you are immediately using the given name. Let's suppose that someone introduces himself to you as Adam. And you say: "Hi Adam, nice to meet you." After a while of conversation, you might ask, "Listen, Adam, you've got a cool accent, are you from...?" Another way to repeat the name is by pronouncing it in your thoughts. In this case, after Adam introduces himself, you say in your head, "Adam, Adam, Adam, Adam, Adam, Adam..." The third possibility is to write this name on a piece of paper as soon as you have the opportunity to do so. Of course, it depends on the circumstances in which you meet, but you can always save that name on your cellphone or somewhere else. The mere act of writing it will help your memory to a great degree.

217

Create Associations

Whenever you hear a new name, create images that include the name's associations with an object or event. Also, make this image vivid, funny, or even absurd and overdrawn, colorful, and in motion—it will make you remember this picture and the name connected with it much better.

A few examples:

You just met Caroline. Imagine her wearing a big, colorful necklace of coral beads. These corals are heavy, have a strange shape and bright colors. She bought this necklace in South Carolina.

You just met Adam. Imagine him dressed as a dignified lady. She wears a long and beautiful dress and has a fan in her hand, which she uses for cooling herself. Now that it's not Adam, you should address him, madam!

Kenny. You just checked your pockets, and you have no cash! You ask Kenny to lend you a penny so that you can grab a nice cold beer together.

Ann. Imagine Ann dressed as a police officer and holding a gun. She has an oversized police hat on her head and a scared robber handcuffed to her wrist. Ann and her big gun.

As you can see, it's pretty simple. Anyone can create such funny or silly associations in a few seconds. When you do this, keep the created image in your head for a few moments. Now, if you have to remind yourself of a particular name, the association will come immediately to your mind.

Note that you can create specific associations with many names. Then, for example, when you meet another Caroline, you will already know which image to use, without a need to create a new one each time. This is a great idea, but since I find it quite amusing to come up with new ideas every single time, I did not decide to do this very often.

Ask Again

If, for some reason, you could not use these techniques or you've somehow already forgotten the name of someone you've just met— don't be afraid to ask them to repeat their name. This person certainly will be happy to tell you their name again. It's a much better solution than allowing for a situation in which you will have to use that name for a few hours, and it's gone from your memory.

You can simultaneously use all of these ideas; however, in most cases, you only need one technique (numbers 3 or 4). Therefore, it is best first to test each of them individually. See which one works best for you and stay with it. Using both repeating and associations is a sure way always to remember new names.

When I meet new people and still chatting, my strategy is to use their name often in conversation and repeat it in my memory. As soon as I finish talking with them and I have a free moment, I create some funny associations in my mind.

When the problem of remembering names is gone, you need to remember one more thing. Use these names! You have to show people that you remember their names. When you ask someone about something, you should use their name as part of the question. If you stopped talking with them and want to ask them about something again, start a sentence by saying their name. As this person hears their name and realizes that you already remember it despite the fact you have just met, it will be a very enjoyable experience for them. You will make a great impression on them, and your conversation will be taken to a completely different level.

Chapter 27: Meeting People

Introducing Self and Other People

When people learn how to introduce themselves and others in informal and formal situations, their confidence level tends to reach new heights. The skills of meeting people and making introductions are the foundation of bringing individuals together. People who have mastered these skills automatically and unconsciously play the host's role wherever they go, which can be quite interesting to watch.

People interact with several different social circles. Many socialize with workplace colleagues, neighbors, family members, and so on. In most cases, people keep their different social circles separate, either unintentionally or intentionally. However, there are many situations where those groups of people will meet, such as parties, funerals, weddings, etc. When this happens, one may have to make numerous introductions.

Introducing Self

People are bound to see someone they do not know, no matter where they go. At a large get-together, party, or formal event, everyone should make the most of the opportunity by introducing themselves to others.

A self-introduction to a new acquaintance is as easy as saying, "Hello, my name is (insert name here). I don't believe we've met." On the other hand, if the person approaching is familiar, using their name will make an individual's introduction a bit friendlier. For example, "Hi Mr. Simons, my name is <NAME>. It's an honor to meet you."

Introducing Others

If the people introduced are of the same gender and age range, it does not matter whose name one says first. However, if they are of different gender but are in the same age group, one should say the female's name first. For example, "Susan, this is my neighbor Paul. Paul, this is Susan." On the other hand, if they have a different age range, it is important to say the older an individual's name first. For example, "Uncle Simon, this is my friend, Ivy. Ivy, this is my uncle, Simon Books." Finally, if one of them is a VIP, his or her name should come first.

Things to Keep In Mind

It is important to remember that when introducing relatives, one should offer their full names. An individual's friends or co-workers would not call an individual's parents "Dad or Mom"; however, they might have to unless one tells them their names.

It is also helpful to add a little more information about that one is introducing. For example, Paul, this is Ivy. She loves hiking too." This gives Paul an excellent conversation starter and or topic, for which he will appreciate it. Also, a firm handshake and friendly smile will win everyone over and make a great impression.

Introducing Other Informal Settings

It is important to use the first and last names when introducing individuals in work and other formal settings. Introductions made informal settings, such as business events, should take rank and position into consideration. One should state the name of the most senior person first. For example, "Mr. Jackson (manager), this is our new Accountant, Samuel Sanders."

When introducing a special benefactor or client, state his or her name first. This applies even if the person to whom one is introducing him or her to have a higher position in an individual's workplace. For example, "Ivy Summers, please meet Professor Paul Strongman, who is our company's President." On the other hand, when introducing equal rank in the academic or corporate world, one should start with the person one knows less well.

Other Things to Keep In Mind

Following the introduction, always continue to address others as Mr. or Ms., unless one is expressly asked to use their first name. However, it is up to one whether to accept the offer or not.

It is important to use an individual's first and last name when introducing oneself.

At dinners or informal settings, the host meets, greets, and introduces people who do not know each other. In networking events, however, people are free to introduce themselves.

Since some people tend to struggle when it comes to remembering names, re-introductions may be necessary.

It is important to make the most out of any introduction opportunity. Meeting a new person can be as fun as opening a gift. A new acquaintance may turn out to be a great client, best friend, or even an individual's future love. The benefits are endless. The only mistake one can make is not introducing self and other people when an opportunity arises.

Proper introductions help make people feel at ease in formal and informal situations, making conversations more comfortable. In other words, introductions aim to allow people to meet someone new. Knowing all the rules of introducing self and other people and all types of introductions should be easy for anyone. Mastering the skill of meeting people can help one look good to those who meet for the first time or introduce it to others.

People Connections

People's connection is simply the process of how human beings link up and form a deep understanding of each other when they realize they share the same goals and vision. People's connections improve our social skills. This skill helps people avoid being anxious or awkward in social setups and instead put themselves out there.

Connecting with people nowadays can be either physically or by using technology. By just clicking a button, one can make new connections on different social platforms. However, the most important and valuable people connections happen face-to-face.

How Do You Meet New People?

To develop this skill, one has to meet new people first. The process of meeting new people can start by just talking to that co-worker you never say hello to or that neighbor you pass every day walking his dog. Attending things like art galleries, book clubs, cooking classes, or music recitals is a good way to meet new people. To meet new people, be open to trying out new things that you would otherwise say no to. When you establish the connections, show genuine interest.

How to Develop People Connection

Many of us struggle to meet people and develop connections with them. If one feels uncomfortable or shy about putting themselves out there, here are seven ways they can improve their people connection skills:

Being a social person: Often, people avoid putting themselves in social situations that will make them feel shy, awkward, or anxious. To connect with others, talk, interact and mingle with people you do not know. Do not let shyness or anxiety hold you back.

Encourage them to talk about themselves - If one lacks this skill, the best way to start developing it is by encouraging others to talk about themselves in social setups. When conversing, show interest in their careers, family, or current events but avoid controversial topics like politics.

Offer flattering remarks - Learn to politely compliment or praise the people you meet on anything they have done or accomplished. If you are from watching them perform, commend them for their performance. This is usually an icebreaker when starting conversations.

Have proper etiquette - Politeness and good manners, in general, helps improve an individual's social skills. When approaching new people, ensure that you maintain proper etiquette; you do not know whom you will meet.

Have a target - Setting a target for yourself is a good way to develop this skill. If your target is to connect with two people per day, strive to talk to at least two people. You can start small then increase the target number when you get more confident.

Be keen on people's body language - One can learn a lot by observing an individual's body language. Be keen to note if your presence is making someone comfortable or uncomfortable and react appropriately. Uncomfortable people will most likely not be open to holding a conversation for too long.

Pay attention - When meeting new people, it is always good to ensure that no distractions interrupt your conversations, like a cell phone that keeps buzzing. Referring back to what they have just said shows you listened and made them want to listen to you even more.

How to Build On the Connections after the First Meeting

After connecting with people in social gatherings, the connection can quickly end as soon as the event is over. However, one can strengthen it by doing the following.

Extend an invitation - Once you establish common interests, be the one to break the ice and invite them for tea or to such-like events. Offer the invitation when winding up on the conversation. You will be surprised how many show up.

Exchange business cards: If it is a business setup, feel free to give out your business card if they want to get in touch with you and politely request theirs.

Attend similar events - The best way to meet someone again after making that first connection is by attending another event similar to the one you initially met. If you met at an art gallery, the chances of bumping into them in another art gallery are quite high.

The Benefit of People Connections

Connecting with others and improving your social skills has the following benefits:

It boasts an individual's self-confidence - Being able to meet, interact, and connect with other people is a sure way of boosting an individual's self-confidence.

Helps build relationships - Making new connections can help build new relationships as well as future friendships. These new connections can open the door to new job opportunities or businesses, new friendships, and help you understand others better.

Improve communication - Connecting with others is likely to help one develop better communication skills. By connecting with many people, one can learn and grow their communication skills.

Helps one become more efficient - By connecting with others, you quickly learn what you like and dislike people and avoid people you do not like.

Not everyone in an event will be interested in connecting with you and vice versa. However, the goal is to focus on your targets and surpass them. Avoid dwelling on any rejections and celebrate any positive connections made.

Making Friends

Making friends is a social skill that everyone has to practice in their lifetime. When young, it was much easier to make friends than as an adult. This is true because kids are not afraid to show vulnerability. They do not dwell too much into what they are ripping out of friendship as adults do. Friends become a big part of our lives. They are the people who will always be there through sad times and happy times. However, there are different types of friends:

Regular friends: One meets these friends every so often to catch up. Conversations with them are usually about regular topics.

Acquaintances - These friends are the ones you meet every day just because you attend the same school or organization. Your conversation with them is usually hi-bye or how you are doing. You never meet them anywhere else.

Best friends: These are your ride or dies, and your conversations are not limited to anything. You trust each other and share very personal information. Even though you may not meet up often, your relationship is solid strong.

Conclusion

For some of us out there, speaking to someone in a casual atmosphere may be easy, while speaking to someone in a more forced social situation may make us more inclined to hide from the world than anything else. There are also instances where we fumble over our words, overact, fidget too much, say inappropriate things, or feel we need to fill the silence by saying something. Or perhaps, it's as simple as being shy or having social anxieties. Learning the basics of communication is only part of your journey to improve your social skills. The other parts are for you to understand what your goals are and for you actually to put them into play.

There are three basic communication areas we'll be going over. These are non-verbal communication, basic social skills, and real-world application. Non-verbal communication normally deals with body language, which accounts for 55% of effective communication. In comparison, the verbal aspect accounts for the other 45% by splitting them into separate categories: the tone of voice and words. Your tone of voice accounts for 38% of effective communication, while the words you and others say are the lowest at only 7%. Now, why do you think that is? Why do you think we pick up on someone's body language and the sound of their voice more than what they're saying?

It's because unspoken forms of communication are universal. They go back before we learned how to talk and when we knew what words were. These are the first things we come to understand at a very young age. When a baby laughs, it must mean it thinks something is funny.

When a baby cries, we instinctively think something is wrong. When we speak lovingly to a baby, they begin to respond not only to the voice but to the action that follows. In short, you can say this has been programmed into us since a very young age. This is something we have taught ourselves to recognize comfort, safety, and nourishment. As this is the very first thing we learned, we unknowingly take any indication of that safety and comfort from the people around us as we get older. We see gestures before we speak. We hear the tone before we listen to words. We understand the other person's message before we get involved with the conversation. By visually assessing and understanding the tone, you get a notion of how this person may feel.

In addition to these non-verbal aspects, there is listening. Listening is a form of communication; however, we'll be focusing on Active Listening. This communication art requires the listener to be engaged in the conversation by having your ears open more so than trying to convey or fill in the silence with words. This is very important to those who are trying to connect. They want someone who is going to listen and understand their message. If you're the quiet type already, then you're already there, not because you're silent, but because you know how to listen and observe overall. Staying silent can tremendously work to your advantage at times when used properly.

To help you build a genuine rapport with others, active listening gives you the advantage of understanding your partner or group members more easily. This opens up opportunities to chime in with some nuggets of wisdom after they're done. This shows others that you're willing to listen to what they have to say, relate, and not judge but help if need be. For you, this builds trust between you and whomever you speak with. However, if you're the nervous type and still find yourself struggling with social situations like these, here's some advice about active listening.

Active Listening is where you listen for the sake of understanding, not for replying. Many people only stay silent to build a rebuttal. Still, if you're trying to get people to like who you are, it's best to understand what they're trying to say instead of spending energy and nerves scrambling for something to say in exchange. You want the others to feel safe around you and open up possibilities to meet up in the future. To be a good listener, don't judge. Let people talk and engage with them in their moments.

As you're listening, take note of how they sound. Do they sound happy? If they do, then perhaps what they're saying is going to lead to something funny? Do they sound disappointed? If they do, then perhaps you should offer some feedback by relating to a similar situation you once experienced? Do they sound irritated? If they do, then perhaps lending some advice to help them see a silver lining will help? Regardless of what you are listening to, always save what you want to say for last. To make sure they're done speaking, just wait for them to fall silent. You can say things like "Well," or "You know what," after you've listened and understood what they were trying to say. As someone meeting others for the first time, don't feel as though you can't say what's on your mind; just remember there are appropriate and inappropriate things that others will either have you liked or ignored.

Let's talk about Body Language again. As mentioned, body language accounts for 55% of effective communication. This is your first step in determining your conversation's direction and even understanding if the other person is engaged or not. This should also be something you're mindful of when speaking to others, too, since you are also part of this conversation and trying to make an impression. A person's body language is based on their personality. For you, you want to use positive body language, not body language that tells others that you're not interested, scared, fidgety, or have anxiety. The non-verbal movements and gestures convey interest, enthusiasm, and positive reactions to what others are saying. If you want to make sure you aren't hurting your chances, try making a checklist of what to look out for.